P9-CRW-751

Kick Up Your Heels . . . Before You're Too Short to Wear Them

Other Hay House Titles by Loretta LaRoche

The Best of Loretta LaRoche (4-CD set)

How to Be a Wild, Wise, and Witty Woman:
Making the Most Out of Life Before You Run Out of It
(4-CD set)

Life Is Short—Wear Your Party Pants:
Ten Simple Truths That Lead to an Amazing Life
(available as a book, 2-CD set, and a DVD)

Relax—You May Only Have a Few Minutes Left:
Using the Power of Humor to Overcome
Stress in Your Life and Work
(book; available February 2008)

Squeeze the Day: *365 Ways to Bring JOY*
and JUICE into Your Life (book)

The Wise and Witty Stress Solution Kit

Kick Up Your Heels . . . Before You're Too Short to Wear Them

How to Live a Long, Healthy, Juicy Life

Loretta LaRoche

HAY HOUSE, INC.
Carlsbad, California
London • Sydney • Johannesburg
Vancouver • Hong Kong • New Delhi

Published and distributed in the United States by: Hay House, Inc.: www.hayhouse.com • ***Published and distributed in Australia by:*** Hay House Australia Pty. Ltd.: www.hayhouse.com.au • ***Published and distributed in the United Kingdom by:*** Hay House UK, Ltd.: www.hayhouse.co.uk • ***Published and distributed in the Republic of South Africa by:*** Hay House SA (Pty), Ltd.: orders@psdprom.co.za • www.hayhouse.co.za • ***Distributed in Canada by:*** Raincoast: www.raincoast.com • ***Published in India by:*** Hay House Publishers India: www.hayhouse.co.in

Editorial supervision: Jill Kramer • *Design:* Nick C. Welch

Library of Congress Cataloging-in-Publication Data

LaRoche, Loretta.
Kick up your heels-- before you're too short to wear them : how to live a long, healthy, juicy life / Loretta LaRoche. -- 1st ed.
p. cm.
ISBN-13: 978-1-4019-0617-7 (hardcover)
ISBN-13: 978-1-4019-0618-4 (tradepaper)
1. Life. 2. Longevity. 3. Aging. 4. Success. I. Title.
BD435.L25 2007
158--dc22 2007008186

Hardcover ISBN: 978-1-4019-0617-7
Tradepaper ISBN: 978-1-4019-0618-4

10 09 08 07 4 3 2 1
1st edition, September 2007

Printed in the United States of America

To my daughter, Laurie,
for her incredible courage,
grace, and dignity.

CONTENTS

Introduction

My great-grandmother Conchetta Sabina is one of the role models for this book. She was a combination of Bette Midler, Rita Moreno, and Emeril: funny, lusty, and fiery! She lived with great passion and was filled with juice and joy. She loved to laugh, dance, and cook; she was spontaneous, compassionate, somewhat eccentric, incredibly irreverent, and open to having a good time. She also had a fantastic sense of humor.

My great-grandmother wore long, flowing dresses but never wore underwear. She probably figured out that if you're in an accident, your underwear isn't going to stay clean for long. When her first husband died, she remarried a man named Peppino, who was 21 years her junior. She always called him *caro,* or "dear one." Peppino was a cobbler and a musician, and he gave Conchetta his handmade shoes and wrote love songs about her, which he lovingly played on his mandolin.

She died on her way to playing cards at the age of 95. She was juicy and knew how to "kick up her heels." I was born shortly after her death and have often wondered if our souls crossed paths and my great-grandmother's energy latched on to me for another ride. My mother frequently remarked how similar we are. Conchetta's nickname was *zingara,* a Sicilian slang word for "gypsy." As a child, my mother always called me by that name and it felt very familiar.

My grandmother Francesca is role model number two. She was patient, caring, loving, and spiritual; she was also a great cook and an incredible martyr. It sometimes seemed as if suffering were her goal. I've often told my audiences that she wore black just in case somebody died.

My mother, Laura, is my third inspiration—feisty, tenacious, bright, and funny. She has always loved to stir the pot. If there was anything brewing in the family, she could make one hell of a stew out of it.

These three Italian divas were my magnificent gene pool, and I'm grateful to them for it . . . every single day.

Chapter 1

A Good Pair of Heels Needs Good Soles

"When it's over, I want to say: all my life I was a bride married to amazement. I was the bridegroom, taking the world into my arms."
— from "When Death Comes," by Mary Oliver

When I reached my 60th birthday, I panicked at the thought that I had less time ahead of me than I had behind me. Of course, that could be debated by those who are seeing from the rear. On a brighter note, this realization enhanced my need to discover as much as I could about the aging process—both the negative and positive. I'm fortunate to have had grandparents who lived long lives, and a mother who's now 96. If genetics are on my side, then I'm in luck.

Like most people, I never really understood or believed that I'd actually reach the same place my mother was many years ago. Not that I would want the alternative, which is not to be here at all. But when she'd try to tell me how she felt about getting older, I dismissed her by saying, "Oh, you have plenty of time." She'd counter with, "You'll see." Well, she was right. I *am* seeing, and it's quite a ride! Bette Davis was right on the money when she said that "old age is not for sissies." I've become a great admirer of my mother's resiliency and all of the other individuals who've become prototypes for my own journey. I'll mention more of these inspirational people throughout the book.

As my mother's body began to betray her by becoming frail, her humor would continue to sustain her. She'd remind me that she had the "furniture disease." When I asked what that was, she quipped, "That's when your chest falls into your drawers." Well, much of what she said is true: Our minds and bodies change, and if we're around long enough, our lives become a roller-coaster ride. If we're lucky, the highs are greater than the lows. But like any ride, we know that someday it will end.

The good news about aging in the 21st century is that many gains have been made in the area of longevity and quality of life. We have a greater understanding of what ages the body and how we influence that process. Not long ago, it was thought that genetics was the primary factor in determining how long we lived and the quality of life we could expect; however, we now know that genes alone aren't something to bank on, especially if we've managed to make more withdrawals than deposits into our life-expectancy account. How we live our lives mentally, physically, and spiritually means much more than we ever imagined.

It seems ludicrous that most people don't think about this until they're quite old or have been diagnosed with some type of physical or mental ailment. In order to have the greatest impact on how we live our later years, we need to think about this much sooner. Unfortunately, most of us are invested in believing we're immortal when we're young, and getting old is the furthest thing from our minds. But it's important to remember that regardless of how long we've waited, it's never too late to start aging well. The body/mind has incredible abilities to repair and restore itself.

With this book, I hope to engage you in the process of living not only longer, but also wiser, healthier, happier, more enthusiastically, and juicier. I love the word *juicy.* I made it part of the book's subtitle because I think it's one of the clearest metaphors for getting through life: When life loses its juice, we begin to wither and dry up. Children are inherently juicy. No one needs to force them to play, laugh, delight in the ordinary, or to be curious or authentic. Kids haven't yet learned to judge, hold grudges, or hang on to anger. And for them, eating is a necessity but not a main focus for their attention, and no one has to prod them into moving their bodies. Unfortunately, as life becomes more involved, sorrow, disappointment, and the constant messages to grow up and be responsible take over our psyches. We lose the succulence of youth in exchange for some of the withering ways of adulthood, and some of us become terminally serious.

I remember going to the market with my grandmother and watching how she always had to squeeze the fruit, insisting that it was the only way to tell if it was ripe with flavor and juice. If it felt hard or scaly, she'd throw it back. Don't we all love biting into a piece of fruit that spurts and squirts and may even spritz juice on those around us? Our lives should be like that. Yes, we have our days or weeks or even years of struggle and strain, but if we can incorporate the tools that I suggest throughout this book, we'll have better skills to navigate the bumps and lumps along the way.

Some of these techniques will be familiar to you, and others will be new. I also hope to reinforce the things you already do that enhance your life. But whether these "juicy tidbits" are just being introduced to you now or you currently use them in your life, the information and skills will be most useful if—like mastering a musical instrument—you simply practice, practice, practice.

Our whole lives have been a practice of one sort or the other—good and bad. Why not leave a legacy for our friends and family of a life well lived?

Juicy Tidbits

- Can you think of someone in your family whose life you find an inspiration, whose wisdom and accomplishments you admire? If so, try to find out everything you can about the person's life.
- Do you resemble the individual—physically, mentally, or spiritually?
- Can you correlate some of your behaviors to ancestors or immediate family?
- Do you see any particular talent or skill that's repeated in yourself or your children?
- Who are the juiciest individuals in your gene pool?
- Have you considered creating a family history to pass down? It's not only an interesting exercise, but one that might save your life or that of someone who's dear to you. Medical conditions can be inherited, and knowing certain information about your ancestors can help your doctor create a better diagnosis.

TRACE YOUR FAMILY TREE FOR FREE!

Want to learn about the ship that your great-grandmother sailed to America on? Try **www.Ancestry.com**, **www.Amiglia.com**, or **www.EllisIsland.org**. You can trace your genealogy online and possibly find other family members to correspond with. If you want to find out where your long-lost relatives live now, go to **www.yourfamily.com/lost_family.html**. Or if you're interested in discovering where your surname came from, check out **www.searchforancestors.com**. Have fun!

"And in the end, it's not the years in your life that count. It's the life in your years."
— Abraham Lincoln

Our greatest assets and strengths in our quest for longevity is our ability to adapt to what's going on with our bodies and our lives. Not being able to change is the death knell of a youthful spirit. Some people are hell-bent on staying the same, and if you suggest something that's different from their usual agenda, they often respond with, "That's not who I am." Well, to those people I say, "Why not put a coffin in your living room to practice being dead, since you're almost there anyway!" In order to thrive and survive, we must become change agents. We also need to increase our spiritual path by learning to forgive the past, love the present, and create a future that resonates with our deepest values. This, my friends, is the primary focus of the book.

In order to understand and take charge of our own situation requires the ability to take stock of our lives in meaningful ways, not only for us but for others as well. That's the definition of wisdom. Yes, wisdom is the result of firsthand experience and learning, but it's much more than that. It's the ability to use the knowledge to positively change ourselves—and by doing so, we consequently contribute to the betterment of society.

Juicy Tidbits

- In an interesting article from the *Authentic Happiness Coaching Newsletter* of the University of Pennsylvania, Ben Dean, Ph.D., examines research on wisdom and its connection to happiness in older adults: "Wisdom is a positive predictor of successful aging. In fact, wisdom is more robustly linked to the well-being of older people than objective life circumstances such as physical health, financial well-being, and physical environment (Ardelt, 1997; Baltes, Smith, & Staudinger, 1992; Bianchi, 1994; Clayton, 1982; Hartman, 2000)."

- Dr. Dan Baker in his best-selling book *What Happy People Know* writes about the scientific side of wisdom and our brains. The more intelligence we seek, the more developed our brain cells will be; that is, more dendrites will form ("branches" that transmit electrical impulses). An "ultimate brain cell" has a sixth branch, which is created and continues to evolve in individuals who have surpassed general facts and knowledge and have attained wisdom:

> Wisdom almost always ushers in happiness, and was recently shown . . . to be the best single predictor for aging well. . . . To grow, a sixth-branch dendrite must be actively searching for knowledge. In this search, it is partly motivated by the pleasure of using strong neuronal connections. But at this mature stage of brain development, which usually occurs in midlife or later, pleasure alone is not always enough to prompt the search. Often, the motivation for growth, at this elevated level of consciousness, is to understand suffering—in hopes of ending it.

Ways to Wither

- Never change! Stay predictable so that everyone around you can set their watch by your behavior.
- Don't do anything physical, and eat to the point of no return.
- Complain a lot about everyone and everything, without doing anything about it.
- Make sure that you're totally invested in your own beliefs so you can open your own temple and be the guru of all knowing.
- Wait to enjoy yourself, putting it off until you don't even remember what made you happy in the first place.

I love to laugh, and I hope you'll see the humor in many of my messages. You get juicier the more you chuckle! Imagine the people who research cardiac function discovering that when you laugh, you release nitrous oxide (laughing gas), which in turn may improve blood flow in capillaries. Their findings promote the fact that laughter may actually lower your risk of heart disease. Studies have recently showed that a fun-packed life—one that includes dancing, solving puzzles, playing a musical instrument, or learning a foreign language—could help prevent Alzheimer's. (Even if you didn't get it, at the very least you might have more to forget.) I wonder if Conchetta is sitting up there on the edge of a cloud, waving her spaghetti spoon like a baton and exclaiming, "Lighten up!"

These days, it seems to me that not a week goes by without a magazine or news show doing a "special report" on aging. Why are they all so interested in this "hot" new topic? Well, one of the biggest reasons is that the baby-boom generation is reaching 60 at the rate of 11,000 a day. These folks have never done anything in a passive way, and they aren't going to take aging lying down. This leaves us with a very interesting phenomenon: We have the boomers who don't want to get old like their parents and a culture that's youth obsessed. It's going to be harder for them to grow old than the previous generations.

It's funny to watch how some people try to avoid the effects of aging. . . . We've seen decades of people run, bike, and aerobicize themselves into a host of physical problems. Statistics show that hip and knee replacements will soon be as commonplace as going food shopping. It might be that older people just used to live with joint pain, and now they have a surgical option to relieve it. But it also seems to me that people of our generations exercised, like much else, to excess, and their bodies are now showing the wear and tear.

I should know—I did everything to excess. I was even an aerobics teacher for quite a while, and I literally pounded my joints into the pavement. But I now have a nice new hip, and who knows what body part might come next? I can't go through any kind of airport screening process without setting off alarms. Today, I consider myself "the most wanded woman in America."

Unlike many of my generation, I didn't become a fanatic about my diet, however. My Italian roots made it too difficult for me to get invested in the spiritual path of deprivation. I just can't buy into the demonization of food that's been going on for the last decade or so. The level of obsessiveness outweighs any positive effects of healthy eating. Many individuals who seek to stay young are now on a quest to find food that's grown organically, hasn't been exposed to unnatural substances, and has been hand-delivered from the farm to the supermarket by 18-year-old virgins.

I agree that it makes perfect sense to try and eat food that's nutritious and healthy, but if you keep attempting to divide foods into "dirty" or "clean," it turns mealtime into a very stressful event. It makes me feel as if I have to take out the vacuum and rubber gloves just to have lunch. How did my grandmother ever make it to 93 consuming "tainted" sausage, salami, and prosciutto?

Her nutritional habits echo those of many Europeans. The so-called French paradox has recently created quite a stir. Researchers studying nutrition were surprised to discover how much cheese and other saturated fats French citizens ate and still managed to maintain their weight. Scientists have attributed a variety of reasons to this anomaly, including the intake of red wine by the French. But by and large, the answer is simple: They eat in moderation and always have someone to sit down at the table with, just as my grandmother did.

Eating alone regularly isn't a healthy option for aging well. Loneliness can foster depression, depression increases the possibility of heart attacks, and heart attacks can kill us. We can all have a cardiac incident, but why have it alone? We have a greater chance of surviving if someone else is around. A recent report shows that more than 25 percent of Americans are lonely, and the kinds of food they eat don't make them feel any more wanted or loved.

Anti-aging enthusiasts have embraced plastic surgery as though going under the knife were as easy as brushing one's teeth, but we've all seen those face-lift advocates who've gone too far and look as if they've gotten stuck in a wind tunnel. There are a plethora of procedures that we can invest in to either spruce ourselves up a bit or make dramatic changes.

Believe me, I've thought about having several. It's pretty bad when your breasts start to spread under your armpits and you need a bra that could double as a condo for a family of seven. What happened to those perky breasts that stood at attention? Well, they're certainly at parade rest now. . . .

There are also creams and hair products that tout their youth-enhancing properties. I could make an elephant's hide look as smooth as silk with all the age-defying serums I've bought for my skin. With failing eyesight, it becomes increasingly more difficult to see the labels on the bottles, so there have been times when I've put conditioner on my face and night cream on my hair—I can honestly say that I got the same outcome.

Others use fashion to upgrade their age. It's all well and good to appear up-to-date, hip, and smart, but if you try to look like the Olsen twins at 60, you may end up looking more like a clown without a circus.

When we're young, we're not gifted with common sense or a real appreciation for the reality that we won't live forever in perfect health. No young person really wants to hear this, because our mentality is geared toward believing in immortality. One of my mother's favorite quotes was by George Bernard Shaw: "Youth is wasted on the young." I can truly say that I get it now.

But then what? If you're like me, you've probably expended a lot of energy blaming yourself, thinking, *If only I had kept a steady weight . . . I should have stuck to doing more yoga . . . If only I had eaten more cauliflower. . . .* But "shoulding" on yourself only makes you feel worse. So what's the point? Better to begin where you are now, and remember, *it is never too late to start aging well!*

Still Kickin'

Why We Love Sophia Loren

Okay, call me superficial if you want, but you have to love Sophia Loren simply because she's magnificently, radiantly, and uniquely beautiful.

No one looks like her . . . and no one has tried. Unlike the rush of actresses trying to copy the iconic looks of great Hollywood beauties such as Marilyn Monroe or Brigitte Bardot, there's never been another Sophia. From her perfect bone structure to her ample curves and impeccable sense of style, she exudes elegance, femininity, and power in a way that few other women do.

She once said of her figure: "Everything you see I owe to spaghetti." I know that feeling!

But what's most extraordinary about Sophia is that her beauty is just as striking now as it was half a century ago. Her regal bearing and elegant style still make her, even in her 70s, a woman of profound sensuality and radiance.

I agree with the archbishop of Genoa, who jokingly said that even though the Vatican is opposed to human cloning, "an exception might be made in the case of Sophia Loren."

Chapter 2

How to Live Like You're Well Heeled

"Our deepest fear is not that we are inadequate. Our deepest fear is that we are powerful beyond measure. It is our light, not our darkness, that most frightens us. We ask ourselves, Who am I to be brilliant, gorgeous, talented, fabulous? Actually, who are you not to be?"
— Marianne Williamson

I've often discussed how in love I am with the concept of having lots of energy. When we live life in balance, we soar and have the ability to not only kick up our heels, but walk in them with confidence and attitude. Our energy levels are the result of a variety of behaviors.

I've always been enthralled with the works of Abraham Maslow, who was considered one of the world's most famous humanistic psychologists. He stated that humans are motivated by needs such as air, water, sleep, sex, and so on; and when they aren't satisfied, then sickness, irritation, or discomfort may follow. These needs make us act to alleviate any deficiencies as soon as possible so that we can establish homeostasis, or balance. In order to move up the ladder to self-actualization—which is the path we all must follow to reach our greatest potential as long as we're on this planet—basic requirements must be met first. But to reach the highest rung, to become everything that one is capable of being, more complex needs also have to be attended to.

However, our culture seems to consistently focus on the bottom rung and neglects the higher steps that lead to full potential. Food and exercise are a necessary part of life, but they don't need the amount of energy that we place on them. The poor souls who live daily waiting for a bowl of rice certainly have every right to concentrate on this basic need since their survival depends on it. The ultimate irony, though, is that we're living in a nation with an abundance of food, so much that the surplus is often sent to the dump, yet there are millions of people starving and millions who struggle with obesity or anorexia. We're obsessed with something so very basic and simple.

Every day a new piece of information comes out on how to lose weight and how to exercise. In the last 20 years, the amount of literature that's been published is mind-blowing. It could cover every inch of the planet! Yet it appears that the more we discuss losing weight and exercising, the fatter we get. I can address some of the basic issues concerning these subjects, but for the most part, I'll only touch upon them to reinforce what we already know and share some new research.

I'm much more interested in getting you to realize that food is a joyful part of life that needs to be shared and enjoyed with others as often as possible, and movement allows you to express freedom and use the space around you in new and exciting ways.

"A musician must make music, an artist must paint, a poet must write, if he is to be ultimately at peace with himself. What a man can be, he must be. This is the need we may call self-actualization. . . . It refers to man's desire for self-fulfillment, namely to the tendency for him to become actually what he is potentially: to become everything that one is capable of becoming. . . ."
— Abraham Maslow

Still Kickin'

Why We Love David Carradine

For many Americans, our first exposure to Buddhist thought and culture was in the classic '70s television series *Kung Fu.* David

Carradine portrayed Kwai Chang Caine, the renegade half-American, half-Chinese Shaolin priest whose soft-spoken manner and ability to keep calm in tense situations were exotic and fascinating. The show was a wacky mix of old West adventure and Asian spirituality, but who didn't fall in love with those flashback scenes of the young Caine trying to "snatch the pebble" from the hand of his master, who affectionately called the boy "Grasshopper"?

But David, who came from a well-known theatrical family, knew nothing about martial arts prior to landing the role. However, getting to know Kwai Chang Caine became very powerful for him, as he went on to become an accomplished student of tai chi and qigong.

Now in his 70s, he's still acting: He recently played the title role in Quentin Tarantino's two-picture epic *Kill Bill* and will be in an upcoming film version of Shakespeare's *Richard III.* He also teaches tai chi; and with the same lean figure he had as a 20-year-old, David remains an athlete of martial arts and has made instructional videos to teach the rest of us the skills that we so loved watching him perform as a young man.

With David Carradine, it's easy to confuse the actor with the character because he gives off the air of a true Shaolin priest who has somehow attained a deeper understanding and an inner peace. And who doesn't love that?

Sizing Things Up

I've watched our society expand more and more over the years. It's an interesting phenomenon considering that the generation following my mother's made jogging and going to the gym almost a religious experience, yet as they've aged, they've added girth at a far greater rate than their parents. Could it be that not having a close community of family members around—old, young, and in-between—starves the soul?

The older generation, like my grandmother's, had no hesitation about pointing out to me (or anyone else) if I was eating too much. They were the standard bearers of wisdom and common sense—something that's sorely missing in our present world. Today we'd call the Department of Social Services and tell them that we're being psychologically abused, or we'd buy a book on how to deal with "difficult" relatives. What's wrong with having people who love us step in with a "reality check," as long as it's done with compassion and kindness?

Another problem is that we've also become excessive in everything, so we struggle with the duality of trying to be healthy and fit while being surrounded by an abundance of foods and all kinds of gadgets that free us from having to physically move. We gorge ourselves on comfort foods because we're so stressed about having to check our e-mail 22 hours a day. If we had to walk to the corner post office to get our mail, at least we'd burn a few calories!

Juicy Tidbits

- Read aloud some items from the menu to your friends while you're out to dinner and it may be one way of "tasting" some of the decadent entrées. If you think of a lemon, your mouth will start to water and feel tangy. Perhaps the same thing could happen if you describe a rich brownie with hot fudge sauce and homemade whipped cream down to the smallest detail. Imagine your mouth filled with the flavors. Think of the calories you'll save.

- Order a few appetizers instead of an entrée. I love the experience of a mini-buffet. Just remember that a few is two, or at the most three, items.

- It's a well-known fact that obesity can take years off our lives, but new research published in *The New England Journal of Medicine* states that being just a few pounds overweight in middle age may also raise the risk of dying earlier. For those who are obese at 50, the odds are more than three times greater. The study was large enough to exclude people who had smoked or had a chronic disease since they can both cause weight loss. The lead author of the study, Michael F. Leitzmann, M.D., of the National Cancer Institute's Division of Cancer Epidemiology and Genetics, strongly suggests that we should strive to maintain a healthy weight throughout life.

- Researchers in the UK examined the tips of chromosomes, or telomeres, which can be read like tiny biological clocks. Each time chromosomes divide, telomeres shorten; therefore, longer tips equal a younger biological age. According to the study, obese women showed an average of 8.8 years more aging compared to their peers with healthy body weights. You want to make those telomeres happy.

- In a recent *New York Times* article discussing research on the links between a restricted-calorie diet and its positive impact on aging, Michael Mason looks at some of the results from scientists: "Extrapolating from recent animal findings, Dr. Richard A. Miller, a pathologist at the University of Michigan, estimated that a pill mimicking the effects of calorie restriction might increase human life span to about 112 healthy years, with the occasional senior living until 140."

When metabolism decreases, it amps up the gene *SIR2,* which has been shown to be linked to longevity. One of the compounds that activates the genes' proteins may be resveratrol, an antioxidant found in red wine. However, it would take a lot of wine to achieve this, so enjoy a glass or two, and don't worry about how long you may live as a result.

- Go ahead and eat a piece of dark chocolate. Recent studies reveal that chemicals contained in this tasty treat help prevent plaque buildup on teeth.

- Take a multivitamin. As people age, their ability to absorb certain nutrients decreases, says Dr. Eileen T. Kennedy, dean of the Friedman School of Nutrition Science and Policy at Tufts University in Boston, Massachusetts. Typical American diets lack magnesium, zinc, vitamin E, and other important nutrients. Kennedy suggests taking a daily multivitamin that has no more than 100 percent of the recommended daily allowance of any nutrient, and only children under 18 and menstruating women should take those that contain iron.

B complex and folic acid become harder for the body to absorb as well, and deficiencies in folic acid have been found to increase levels of the amino acid homocysteine, which can increase the risk of heart attacks. Also, to enhance calcium absorption, be sure to get at least 600 to 800 milligrams of vitamin D daily.

Visualize a pie and then imagine all the pieces of your life. Where do you put your energy? What has the biggest slices of the pie?

- Self-care
- Family
- Friends
- Children or Grandchildren
- Work
- Home
- Leisure
- Volunteering
- Hobbies
- Daydreaming

If you're spending too much time taking care of other people or being a busy adult who works 24/7, you need to switch gears and find some balance.

"Never eat anything larger than your head."
— Miss Piggy

I'm sure that by the time I get to the end of my life, scientists will come up with a formula that will allow us to eat as much as we want and not get fat, or all the rats that they've used for research will be very svelte. I'm sick to death of hearing about dieting! If I have the opportunity, I'm going to write a book on weight loss and exercise called *Laugh Your Ass Off.* No one has managed to combine eating with fun. It's become dreadfully serious, and I'm certain that this isn't good for our health or mental well-being. As a matter of fact, it's not as silly as it might sound: Hearty laughter burns up to 40 calories in 15 minutes and increases metabolism by 10 to 20 percent. We could be looking at four pounds a year. More important, the pleasure, joy, and company of those we care about is where true nourishment resides.

"A Tavola Non S'invecchia"

There's a wonderful Italian saying, *a tavola non s'invecchia,* which translates as "at the table one never grows old." My fondest memories are recalling family time at the dinner table, eating, laughing, and oohing and aahing over everything placed before me. No one ever ate alone or multitasked while eating. Why isn't anyone gushing about their meals anymore? Why have we lost the ability to see food as a great source of pleasure? When we eat, we should act as if we've been given a blessing. Who knows if our cells just might be listening to what we're saying and then giving us what we think we deserve.

Don't attach negative connotations to your meals. If you've overeaten or had too many fatty, rich, or sugary foods during the day, just accept it and move on. You can make corrections the next time. Nobody, including you, needs to hear over and over how disgusted you are with yourself, how bloated you look, or how little self-control you have. It doesn't serve you in any positive way, and it's incredibly boring to everyone around you.

I'm a big believer in the power of common sense, which is probably why a friend shared with me that my success was due to the fact that I have a fantastic natural bullshit detector. I'm often blown away because the stuff people blindly accept about health and happiness is so fabricated that the original fabric seems to have disappeared.

I think I inherited the trait from my grandmother, who definitely had Sicilian intuition. She was a bemused skeptic and never would have sat in front of the tube believing some of the ridiculous information that's presented by the diet gurus, who travel the media circuit selling their books and potions. Yet we then run out to purchase one useless book after another. We're out 20 bucks, and the author accumulates royalties and buys a house in the Caribbean while we remain fat and unhappy.

We all know how to lose weight: Eat less and move more. What we haven't understood is the inherent need for all humans to break bread together. When we gather with one or more to eat and share our day—or any number of situations—we're following our tribal heritage. We were meant to live in community, but our culture continues to deny this most important need in lieu of completing our to-do lists. We've exchanged efficiency for the benefits of being with each other, but as we age, the latter becomes more and more important. We need to be seen, heard, and understood in a setting that allows this type of interaction without the distraction of a cell phone ringing or a pager buzzing.

I've often been in the company of individuals who feel compelled to take every call even in the midst of a conversation. They leave their BlackBerry on the table and stare at it intermittently while periodically looking at me. My grandmother would have gone berserk and yelled several curse words as she threw the thing in the trash—no one messed with Nonna. Today, we simply roll our eyes and accept that what's going on is "business as usual," when in fact, it's simply *rude.*

Eating while you're driving, sitting at your desk, or walking down the street is like being hypnotized. It's pretty hard to discern how much or even what you're consuming while you're doing something else. No one tries to have sex while they're ironing or shingling a roof (but I'd bet it's been done). Why take one of life's true nurturing pleasures and make it an "add on" to the more mundane requirements of everyday living? If you really want to live a long, juicy life, then it's important to have as much culinary collaboration as possible. Begin to look at your eating behavior, and check out the following:

Ways to Wither

- Don't sit down to eat. Walk around the house or office while you multitask.
- Leave the cell phone on during every meal as if you were a trauma surgeon.
- Devour your food as quickly as possible so you can get on with more important business.
- Order lots of takeout, especially the kind that goes down easy and doesn't take much chewing.
- Talk about how many calories you've ingested while you're eating and whether the food is good or bad for you. Make anyone who's with you feel guilty and unhappy.

Juicy Tidbits

- Start a cooking club, and give it a quirky name like "The Winning Whisks" or "The Pots and Plans."

- Have your grandchildren, significant other, or anyone close to you who's interested be part of the meal preparation—chop, sauté, and simmer together. It's a great way to create community and continuity with family and friends; and besides, they may be taking care of you someday and you'll want them to know what you like to eat.

- Take a cooking class, but not something ordinary. Learn how to make Thai food or sushi. We have lots of taste buds on our tongues that get bored with the same old fare. It's also a great way to expand your mind in a more global fashion. You'll discover new cultures and perhaps be stimulated to want to go even further, such as taking an exotic vacation.

- Cook a meal for friends or neighbors and bring it over to them. Remember when that was par for the course when you moved into a neighborhood?

- Hire a chef for the night, invite a few friends over, and ask them to chip in. Who knows—you may be able to start your own "in house" cooking show. Do it once a month and videotape the event.

- Try this great idea from a recent issue of *USA Weekend:*

> Consider starting a dinner co-op. By exchanging home-cooked, frozen meals, members can enjoy tasty dishes with minimal hassle. Use [fresh] ingredients whenever possible, shop locally and freeze portions in ziplock bags. Each participant brings two frozen servings per person, plus extra for "tasting" during a freewheeling social hour.
>
> Members dish out $80 to $95 per month, depending on the recipes.

- Create a family cookbook. Gather recipes from as many relatives as possible, and ask if anyone has some from several years ago. What a fabulous heirloom to hand down to future generations! I have my grandmother's cookbook, which must be at least 70 years old now. Every time I look at it, I see her sitting in her chair turning the pages.

Here's one of my favorite recipes that my grandmother made. It was so delicious that I thought I'd swoon from the joy it brought to my taste buds. It's called caponata (sweet-and-sour eggplant stew), and you can eat it as a side dish or as an appetizer on some wonderful bread.

Caponata

Ingredients

Olive oil, extra virgin please!

3 large eggplants, cut into 1" cubes

1 large onion, minced

3 cups tomato sauce (homemade if possible)

¾ cup pitted and chopped green olives

½ cup capers, rinse well

1 cup thinly sliced celery hearts, including a handful of chopped leaves (the leaves have a lot of flavor)

3 or 4 anchovy fillets, minced (if you hate them, leave them out)

About ½ cup red-wine vinegar

About 1 tbsp. sugar, salt, and ground pepper

Heat a half inch of olive oil in a large frying pan, and fry the eggplant in batches until it's golden brown on all sides. Add more oil to the pan as needed. Drain the fried eggplant on paper towels.

In a large, heavy-bottomed saucepan or pot, heat another ½ cup of olive oil and sauté the onion for five minutes, stirring often. Add the remaining ingredients and the drained eggplant; combine gently but thoroughly and simmer over low heat for 30 minutes, stirring occasionally. Taste for seasoning. The caponata should have a pleasant sweet-and-sour flavor.

Transfer the caponata to a large bowl and let it cool. Serve at room temperature. Eat it on some delicious Italian bread or by itself. Share it with friends and family. You'll all feel juicy and joyful after enjoying this fabulous dish!

Above all, learn to savor your food; and don't hurry through anything, even if it's beef jerky. Let the flavors saturate your palate every time you put something into your mouth. If you learn this skill, you'll eventually discover the ability to become satiated more easily.

When we're gulping and wolfing down our food, we can't help not being satisfied—and then we eat more to make up for the lack. Ultimately, we might as well be grunting and snorting in the wild with the rest of the animals.

Chapter 3

Heel, Toe, and Around We Go

"The word 'aerobics' came about when the gym instructors got together and said: 'If we're going to charge $10 an hour, we can't call it jumping up and down.'"
— Rita Rudner

Exercise! How many times a year do you hear the call to action? No one needs to be told to move, yet barely 23 percent of the population does anything beyond what an invalid is able to do. Toilets even flush themselves now—I'm waiting for a hand to pop out and serve up the toilet paper.

Society is lazy, despite the fact that studies on aging regularly show that if there's an elixir resembling the fountain of youth, it's exercise. I want to stress how vital it is to make physical activity an important part of your life; however, my wish is that you'll use it as a way to return to the joys of childhood, as you once skipped, jumped, or freely spun around a room. If you think of exercise as a horrible chore, it *will* be.

I can't remember a time when I didn't love to dance. My mother always told me that I seemed to be doing the rumba when she was pregnant with me. I can honestly say it's one of the things that makes me feel like I was injected with a powerful mind-altering drug: I become one with the music, losing myself completely, and I can sense this same feeling while watching others move with the beat. Since the beginning of time, tribes have had ritualistic dances ingrained into their culture. I believe that we were all born to love rhythmic movement. I think that's why the show *Dancing with the Stars* is such a hit.

A lot of people stop exercising because boredom starts to erode their spirit. You can't keep doing the same routine day in, day out and expect your mind/body to look forward to it. "The physical and mental challenge of shifting among a variety of activities may be protective because it keeps more parts of the brain busy," says Constantine Lyketsos, M.D. The more new things you try, the more benefits you'll receive. With that in mind, I'm going to share some interesting data on exercise and offer up a bunch of juicy ways to let your inner kid come out and play.

Healthful Tidbits

— Statistics show that 70-year-old men who start strength-training programs in middle age and continue to practice it regularly are just as strong, on average, as 28-year-olds who don't exercise. Women who lift weights increase bone density, have fewer falls, and are less likely to fracture their hips.

— Several new studies have revealed that regular, energetic workout routines may prevent or temporarily stall the onset of Alzheimer's disease and will at least curb the bouts of forgetfulness that are typical as we age. In a fascinating article published in a recent *AARP Bulletin,* John Hanc explores more connections that scientists have made between exercise and mental agility: "In a paper published in October [2005], researchers from the Karolinska Institute in Sweden found that those who had engaged in robust physical activity at least twice a week since their youth or middle age had a 50 percent lower chance of developing dementia and a 60 percent lower risk of developing Alzheimer's than those who were sedentary." Interestingly, the countries that are the happiest are also among the fittest. They are Sweden, Norway, Iceland, and Finland—America comes in 23rd. Movement and happiness seem to be a good marriage.

— How about having more money during your later years? Julie Appleby highlights the cost benefits of living an active lifestyle in a *USA Today* article:

> For the cost of a walk a day, you might be able to put off or avoid altogether taking blood pressure drugs or cholesterol medications, for which you could spend $50 to $100 or more a month. Avoid developing diabetes, . . . and you could see much bigger savings. . . . The cost per person averages more than $13,000 a year. And if you can stave off dementia and live on your own longer, you can avoid the $70,000 or more a year that nursing homes cost.

— A study performed by Dr. Patricia McKinley of McGill University in Montreal demonstrated that when seniors danced the tango, there were benefits not only to the body, but also to the brain. Participants had increased muscle tone and balance, but what's more interesting is that their memories improved, and they also showed a greater ability to multitask—on or off the dance floor.

— Keep in mind that too much exercise can hamper your immune response. Remember that moderation is the key!

Juicy Tidbits

Boxing: I wish I had thought about this when I was younger, because I can think of a few people whom I would have punched out. Trainers report that there's a growing interest in boxing among older women in the United States. They take up the sport for a variety of reasons—the main one being fun. You can use boxing moves to get a vigorous workout without ever stepping into the ring. That's always a possibility, though . . . what a great way to dissipate a hot flash! Check out **www.boxingyms.com** to find a trainer and a list of gyms in your area.

Nia: This is a dynamic cardiovascular workout that stimulates and integrates your mind, body, and spirit, leaving you recharged, rejuvenated, and fully alive. Nia blends dance, martial arts, and healing arts (such as yoga) in order to allow your inner child, athlete, warrior, and dancer to emerge. Read more about this fascinating movement at **http://nianow.com**.

Tai chi: If you're interested in a gentler form of martial arts, then tai chi is for you. It's meditative but very physical. Tai chi is gaining popularity and can be incredibly beneficial for balance, and it's excellent for combating osteoarthritis. Regularly engaging in this ancient Chinese discipline may lower blood pressure, increase bone density, and reduce stress. I love the way it looks—like a dance in slow motion. It also has a spiritual side that says to "keep in the flow."

Creative Movement: Put on whatever kind of music you enjoy—classical, jazz, rock and roll, disco, hip-hop—and just act out what you hear. Be zany, childlike, sophisticated, cool, or any other emotion that you're feeling. Imagine a scene from a movie, book, or your own life and become your own drama queen. You may even want to do this with your friends. Invite them over and have each person interpret the music in their own fashion, and then try to guess the emotions behind the dance. This could make for a very cathartic evening!

Trampoline: Bouncing seems to feel good to everyone. We've all done it as kids on the forbidden bed. How many of us have heard a parent shout, "Don't jump on the bed!" Well, this could be catch-up time. A trampoline can provide an aerobic workout without straining joints; however, it takes balance to use it, so be careful.

Tango: I have every intention of learning the Argentine tango. It's a very sexy dance. I can imagine myself in a black dress with a thigh-high slit and red high heels, gliding across the floor with a handsome guy. . . . There are tours to Argentina that include tango lessons where you can learn *el alma* *del tango,* the "soul of the tango." Take a look at this Website to see some of the steps: **http://home.att.net/~larrydla/basics_1.html**.

Counting Steps: Buy a pedometer and find out just how many steps you take in a day. You may be shocked by how little you move! *The Step Diet Book,* by James O. Hill, Ph.D.; John C. Peters, Ph.D.; and Bonnie T. Jortberg, M.S., R.D., comes with a step counter. Walking is an exercise that everyone can do and is a healthy, effective way to lose weight. I think it makes a lot of sense to track your steps, and it enables you to compete with yourself.

And for the more adventurous exercisers among you, try some of these strenuous and fun workouts. They'll keep you healthy and engaged!

Gyrokenesis: Developed by Juliu Horvath and incorporating key principles of dance, yoga, gymnastics, and tai chi, gyrokenesis is a practice that gently stretches joints and muscles through rhythmic and fluid movements. This workout stimulates the processes of internal organs and relaxes and invigorates the total body. For more information, visit **www.gyrotonic.com**.

Kettlebell Training: Russian kettlebells look like cannonballs with handles, and some say that working out with them delivers the most efficient way to get into shape. Russian weight-lifting legends and soldiers of the Special Forces have been using this technique for decades, and now it's available at many health clubs. To find out more about training with them, visit **www.russiankettlebells.com**.

Capoeria: Capoeria is a Brazilian sport that's been around for more than 400 years. Combining dance, music, and martial arts, it's like an elegant form of boxing set to sexy Brazilian music. Find out more at **www.capoeirista.com**.

BalleCore: A blend of yoga, Pilates, and ballet, BalleCore incorporates a challenging, precise, and elegant workout with music that focuses on strengthening the body's core and building cardio fitness. For more information and to read about its founder, Molly Weeks, check out **www.ballecore.com**.

Still Kickin'

Why We Love Twyla Tharp

If you love the art of dance and movement, you have to admire Twyla Tharp. For over 30 years, she has been creating the most innovative, complex, and virtuosic choreography of our times. Her style is no one's but her own; and she continues to fuse classic ballet and contemporary jazz movements into something new, fresh, and exciting.

She performed until the age of 52, but now she leaves the dancing to the youngsters and concentrates on her creations. Her work includes amazing full-length Broadway shows, such as the award-winning and long-running musical *Movin' Out,* based on the songs of Billy Joel; and in 2006, she debuted *The Times They Are A-Changin',* a story told using the music of Bob Dylan.

Twyla is known to be a perfectionist, which scares some people, but I think when someone's work is as brilliant as hers, they're entitled to be as inflexible and demanding as they like. It's hard work and passion that create great art—not compromise. And you have to marvel at her love for the art of dance and appreciation of the power of the human body that's so clearly demonstrated through the joyous movement of her talented dancers.

Rent the film version of the musical *Hair* and watch the opening number, "Aquarius." Even though it's now close to 30 years old, you'll be amazed at the beauty and freshness of Twyla's choreography. Enjoy!

Chapter 4

Don't Wear Out Your Heels

"For fast-acting relief, try slowing down."
— Lily Tomlin

Nothing ages you faster than too much stress. It can create inflammation in the body, which triggers a host of diseases or aggravates preexisting conditions. Have you ever noticed that you look older after enduring a long bout of problems, either at home or at work? I can actually *see* in my face how rested I am once I've been home for a few days after being on the road. Flying, staying in hotels, and dashing here and there take their toll on me; and no matter how much I love my work, it requires much more vigilance and effort than hanging out in a robe and sipping a cup of coffee, knowing that there's nothing pressing for me to do.

The word *stress* is so overused that it has become the definition for anything and everything that doesn't fit the way we want things to be. Over the past 30 years, our lives have become more and more complex, and we don't know how to manage them. We're on call 24 hours a day! We may still be raising children or caring for aging parents, and we must also find time to attend to our own needs. To top it off, we're overwhelmed with the anxieties caused by complicated electronic devices we count on but that often don't work. . . . It's no wonder we all feel constant pressure.

There are options that can make life easier, but they're rarely taken seriously. Why not? I'm convinced it's because stress has become an addiction. Don't you find that when you try to have a conversation with most people, the first thing everyone shares is how much they've been doing since they woke up and they're so busy their heads are spinning? It's as if they've gotten on a runaway bus and are helpless to pull the cord so they can get off.

This is emotionally similar to being on a substance that gives you a high but then makes you its slave. The chemistry of stress can initially give you a rush; but after a while, it begins to erode your body, mind, and soul. And like an addict, you start to *need* it.

I've written about this subject for several years, as have many others; in fact, I'd venture to say that not a day goes by without some media piece focused on the issue of stress management. What I've come to realize is that our society has not only gotten used to the fast pace and pressure of our frantic lifestyle, but we secretly fear that we may lose it. There's something easier about having every moment of our lives already scheduled. We become mesmerized and then don't have to make any decisions or focus on what's really important to us.

The true nature of stress is still misunderstood by the masses. Not everything is stressful, but if we were to eavesdrop on a million conversations across America, we'd start to believe that a pimple is just as much a cause of anxiety as a car accident.

Believe it or not, good stress does exist. It's what gets us up in the morning, urges us to take out the garbage so seagulls don't move in, and helps make our lives interesting and vital. It enables us to perceive the things that need to be managed versus the things that don't. And it keeps us safe in moments of danger.

Distress is bad stress, but much of it is in our power to control. It can happen not only when we react negatively to an event, but to our perception of what may go wrong in the future—and that's something most of us do many, many times a day. It's our heart rate going up when we're in a hurry and see a traffic light changing, it's someone trying to cut in line in front of us at the supermarket, and it's our airline flight that's cancelled at the last minute. Are all of these inconveniences? Yes. But are they life shattering? No! If we were calm and thinking in a rational way, would it really be necessary to have a deeply negative reaction to any of these scenarios?

I'll never forget being at the airport in Toronto waiting to fly back to Boston, when the gate agent suddenly announced that the flight had been delayed. Almost instantaneously, the entire group started acting like a bunch of bulls who had just seen a fertile cow walk by. They all began pawing the earth and snorting, whipping out their cell phones and calling as many people as they could to share this enormous transgression. I realize that there were probably some calls that had to be made, but most individuals can't seem to adjust to a minor irritation without sharing it with the world. Once while I was standing in line at the supermarket, the woman in front of me who was already paying for her groceries called someone to say how aggravated she was about having to wait in a long line. She definitely needed a reality check.

How often do you overreact? How does it feel . . . and what's the point?

I imagine right about now you may be jumping out of your skin, thinking, *What is she talking about? Does she realize that I'm taking care of my elderly parents (or that I'm diabetic, or that I just lost my job)?* Yes, I do understand. I know that taking care of aging parents can incredibly compromise the immune system of the caregiver, and I have complete empathy for this situation and the hundreds of others that you face day in and day out.

In today's world, many of us are multitasking and juggling various aspects of caretaking—while dealing with getting older ourselves. Even though my mother is in an excellent nursing home, not a day goes by that I don't feel some guilt about it. I've spoken to individuals who have a parent living at home, and they also feel guilty. We really haven't figured this out yet. In addition, it's been shown that those who have spent years caring for parents who suffer from dementia age more rapidly than the rest of the population—sometimes up to ten years faster. However, we still have a lot more control over how we handle these situations and our emotional lives than we realize. This is one of the most difficult concepts to understand. Our minds have the power to make life a horror show, or it can choose to make it a haven for tranquility.

Our biology plays a part in this to a degree. Some of us instinctively know how to turn the heat down to a simmer or shut it off completely, while others are born with the heat constantly on high because they're always stirring the pot. The women in my family are anxiety mavens: My grandmother, mother, daughter, and I have all had panic attacks during different periods of our lives. Our brains are just wired to excessively ruminate. I picture it like a dog with a bone—we just can't stop chewing on something.

Women are masters at this. We have an incredible ability to remember past events, as if we have a camera located somewhere midbrain that snaps photos and stores them for later use. When a situation reminds us of something that has already occurred, we're able to recall all the pertinent details with incredible accuracy, usually to the chagrin of the males or children in our lives. Unfortunately, we seem to focus much more intently on the bad stuff than the good.

Is there anyone out there who hasn't been amazed by a mother's ability to recall days and times when her child displeased her, as if she were in charge of the archives at the Smithsonian? The down and dirty of all this is that we'll start to look like Frankenstein (or his bride) if we don't somehow come to the realization that it's up to us to monitor our stress levels.

I don't know about you, but it's pretty exciting to me to understand that I *do* have some control over how I think about things. (I'll talk more about thoughts and their effect in the next chapter.)

Still Kickin'

Why We Love Joan Borysenko, Ph.D.

I first met Joan Borysenko more than 20 years ago when I was running a small wellness institute outside of Boston and hired her to do a seminar. It was early in her lecturing career—mine hadn't started yet—and I'll never forget that at the end of a long weekend seminar with many speakers, Joan spoke up to the participants and said, "The one who should be talking is Loretta!"

I don't know how true that was at the time, but it illustrates the wonderful graciousness of Joan, a woman whose accomplishments are amazing by anyone's standards. She attained her doctorate in medical sciences at Harvard Medical School, where she also completed postdoctoral fellowships in cancer research, behavioral medicine, and psychoneuroimmunology. In addition, she's a licensed psychologist and was the co-founder and former director of mind-body clinical programs at Beth Israel Deaconess Medical Center, a teaching hospital of Harvard Medical School. She has written 13 books—most of them bestsellers—and is widely recognized as a pioneer in the subjects of mind-body medicine and women's health.

She's a very funny and articulate speaker whose passion for bringing science, medicine, and spirituality together to promote health and healing is truly enlightening and inspirational.

Now that we live on different sides of the country, Joan and I don't see each other as often as we used to, but we're sisters in a way. We can talk to one another in a manner that few can appreciate, especially about living the life of a female public speaker who spends much of her time on the road. For her deep spirituality and understanding, I lovingly refer to her as *your Holiness,* and Joan has dubbed me the *Jolly Lama.*

But Joan's real gift is the profound wisdom and insight that she gives to all of us. In my mind, I carry around many of her great sayings and would love to share this one: "Some tension is necessary for the soul to grow, and we can put that tension to good use. We can look for every opportunity to give and receive love, to appreciate nature, to heal our wounds and the wounds of others, to forgive, and to serve."

To me, that's more than enough reason to love Joan Borysenko!

Ways to Wither

- Ignore all physical and mental symptoms such as: not being able to sleep; feeling irritated all the time; overreacting to the noise that the dog makes while he's drinking water; talking too much; feeling sweaty or clammy; experiencing little or no enjoyment; hurrying from one thing to another; twitching, fidgeting, and feeling restless or anxious; and not being able to look in the mirror because you resemble yourself 20 years hence.

Juicy Tidbits

1. Become a contrarian. This is one who bases his or her lifestyle on personal choice and taste, not on the preferences of the crowd. For example, just because everyone around you has schedules bursting with business meetings doesn't mean that you're a loser if you choose to take an hour to read, get a massage, or have lunch with a friend.

2. Realize that when you're stressed, you begin to seize up. Your muscles contract (including your butt cheeks) and soon the tightness travels upward until your lips start to purse. I call this *sphincter-izing*. It results in the catchall phrase for anything perceived as stressful: "Oh no!" Try this instead: Rather than seizing up, purse your lips and keep repeating, "Oh no!" If you say it with intention a few times, it gets incredibly funny—especially for those events that aren't crisis driven. It becomes even more humorous when you do it with a friend or someone at work. It helps you "snap out of it" and move on to solutions and an "Aha!" instead.

3. Understand that you don't have to know everything about everything. Just because the technology exists to access what the weather is in Outer Mongolia, it doesn't mean that you must look it up unless you're packing a bag to go there tomorrow. All that you need to know is where to find the information when you really need it.

4. Give it a rest . . . your mind, body, soul, and your cell phone. Never has so much been said about so little. It *is* possible to wait in line or sit in traffic and not call family members or friends to report in. Do they really need to add your information to their day?

5. Make contact with real people. I always tell my audiences that the real reason the series *Friends* was so popular is because no one has any. Loneliness is on the list of top-ten stressors. More people live alone in America than at any time in history; and for many, TV shows and Internet chat rooms are becoming the substitute for the relatives and neighborhood characters that should be part of everyone's lives, day and night. We need experiences with *real* people in order to live a rich life.

6. Volunteer. Go out and do something for someone else. When you get into a place of thinking that life is too difficult, believe me, there's always someone out there who's in worse shape. Connecting and helping those who are less fortunate gives you a reference point for your own stuff. It's like the old saying: "I cried because I had no shoes until I met a man who had no feet."

7. Identify ten things that would cause you excessive grief and horror. For example, you could write down the loss of a parent, child, or significant other; your home burning down; losing your job; and so on. Put the list somewhere visible, and refer to it whenever you start to make something worse than it really is. It becomes the proverbial dope slap.

8. Have fun. It's one of the best anecdotes to stress. Don't wait to play—play along the way. Don't make everything into an emergency unless you're an ER physician. (And trust me, they have unbelievable skills in this area.)

9. Get help if you need it. Even ordinary, everyday experiences can feel like you're hauling 50-pound bags of concrete through mud when you're suffering from anxiety or depression. As you age, it becomes increasingly difficult to rebound from life's inevitable blows. I've been through some major periods of anxiety; and without a doubt, it's one of the most difficult things to overcome. It's not something that you can simply tell your mind to stop doing. There are prescription drugs on the market now that can really help, but I also believe that medication alone isn't the answer. It's necessary to see what's feeding the negative emotions. What messages do you send yourself? Find a therapist with expertise in the area of cognitive-behavioral therapy who can help you reframe your internal dialogue so you can positively transform your life.

10. Focus on your heart. The Institute of HeartMath is an organization that looks at the scientific link between heart and mind and suggests ways to reduce stress. Their techniques are used by hundreds of thousands of people worldwide and more than 100 organizations, from global corporations to hospitals, government agencies, and schools. HeartMath research suggests that meditation is much more effective when the exercise is geared toward the heart rather than the mind. Learn more at **http://www.heartmath.com**.

In the meantime, try this quick meditation:

- Sit quietly in a place where you won't be disturbed. Focus on your heart and picture it beating in your chest. If your mind wanders, keep bringing it back to your heartbeat.

- Imagine that your breathing is centered in your heart. Slowly inhale, hold it for several seconds, and then exhale. Continue doing so while imagining your breaths coming in and out of your heart.

- Keep practicing this breathing; now recall a time when you felt good, and try to reexperience the moment. Visualize the place and the people you were with, recapturing the event with as much detail as possible. Specifically try to re-create the positive emotions, but if that's too difficult, find a sincere attitude of appreciation. Continue to focus your thoughts and breathing, and you'll feel contentment and relaxation washing over you.

11. Contemplate. Contemplative meditation is a mental device to alter consciousness. It can move beyond mental habits that repeatedly cause you to misinterpret yourself and your world through perception, interpretation, and recollection. The Sufi tradition says: "To awaken in life we first must awaken beyond life."

To begin, focus a meditation session on a single thought, question, or emotion. The intense concentration can often bring clarity. You may spend 30 minutes contemplating the meaning of forgiveness or gratitude, or you may spend it pondering questions such as "Where should I be headed?" Some forms of prayer are, in effect, types of contemplative meditation. (For more on this and related subjects, take a look at *Contemplative Science: Where Buddhism and Neuroscience Converge,* by B. Alan Wallace.)

12. Connect to the flow with qigong. Life's vital energy (chi) flows through the body and keeps you healthy; and when it becomes blocked by stress, injury, or tension, pain and disease can likely result. Qigong is a 5,000-year-old practice that has been proven to stimulate the harmonious flow of chi and enhance physical, mental, and emotional well-being. Practicing qigong regularly can help open the pathways of your body that will allow your life energy to flow freely, activating your body's innate ability to heal itself. Read more about this at the Qigong Institute's Website: **www.qigonginstitute.org**.

The Gratitude Exercise

Sit with a family member, friend, or co-worker and take turns telling each other what makes you feel grateful for having that person in your life. Say nothing while the other speaks, and just feel the warmth and love that comes from someone's heart space. You may even want to record it for future use. These precious moments can relieve anxiety and improve immune function, but more important, they'll allow you to realize that life has more to offer than the constant stress and pressure you perceive to be surrounding you.

Chapter 5

Sole Talk

"Every one is bound to bear patiently the results of his own example."
— Phaedrus (ca. 15 B.C.–ca. A.D. 50)

You can suck the living hell out of the day-to-day by the descriptions you use to discuss—or even to just think about—people, places, events, and yourself. Or you can live as if your cup were half full. How cognizant you are of what you say is directly correlated to the outcome you'll get. If you continually speak of your life in terms that describe it as if you *never* feel good, things *never* turn out right, or *nothing* positive comes your way, you'll more than likely end up being right.

It takes less energy to feel good than it does to feel bad. In fact, I'd go so far as to say that it takes courage to be happy. My great-grandmother Conchetta suffered many indignities and tragedies throughout her life, yet not a day went by without her announcing that she felt blessed with *abbondanza,* "abundance."

You can choose to take all of your experiences and channel them into a reality show based on fear and anxiety, or you can think of all difficulties as opportunities for creating something new.

Negativity is like a big black hole with slippery sides. Once you fall in, it takes a lot of effort to crawl back up. There are also many people who like the security of the darkness, so if you're down there, you'll have lots of company. However, when you decide to come back into the light, they won't help because they're stuck in the quagmire of goo at the bottom, and they want you there with them, too. When you find yourself in a hole, *stop digging!*

It takes vigilance to be the guardian of thoughts, words, and deeds; and you're often at the mercy of years of conditioning that make you operate as if you were on autopilot. The Buddhists say that "all suffering of mankind is produced by attachment to a previous condition of existence." When you use language such as "if only," "I wish," or "I can't," you're dismissing the possibility of today in order to maintain the familiarity of the past or to assuage a fear of the future. You may think it's easier to stay in an unhappy relationship or job or maintain habits that don't serve you, but ultimately you'll suffer the consequences.

In order to be happy, upbeat, and successful, you need to become an actor or actress who has been given a juicy script. Become the character as you read the uplifting lines. For a while, you might not believe the things you say—or you might feel uncomfortable talking about the positive and reassuring aspects of life—because the negative side is safe and strangely comforting. But the more you practice and get into the skin of your "character," the words will flow more naturally until they eventually *become* the way you speak and feel.

Still Kickin'

Why We Love Naomi Judd

On her Website, Naomi Judd says this about herself: "I'm a communicator whether I'm expressing myself through writing a song or a book or I am singing, acting, speaking at an engagement or even chatting one-on-one with a stranger on the street. Finding a way to share our common experiences is my grand passion."

That's reason enough to love her! And isn't sharing common experiences what life is all about?

But then there's the way that Naomi does it. Once a welfare mother living without medical insurance, she was also a victim of domestic violence but somehow managed to overcome her difficulties and become one of the world's most successful entertainers. Listen to some of the songs she recorded with her daughter Wynonna—in particular the

smash hit "Love Can Build a Bridge," and you'll see why she's beloved by millions.

In 1991 Naomi was diagnosed with hepatitis C, a chronic liver disease that forced her to retire from performing. Some people would just lick their wounds in defeat in the face of such a challenge, but for Naomi, her illness opened a whole new life. After treatment for the disease—from which she says she's been cured—she's now turned her focus toward humanitarian efforts. She started the Naomi Judd Education and Research Fund that works to raise awareness of hepatitis C, she's a spokeswoman for the American Liver Foundation, and she sits on the board of Mothers Against Drunk Driving. In addition, every year she returns to her hometown of Ashland, Kentucky, for the Judd's Annual Food Drive, which helps bring needed sustenance to families in the region.

She recently began hosting a television talk show, *Naomi's New Morning,* which focuses on issues of spirituality and personal growth . . . continuing her efforts to reach out to people in need.

Naomi says, "I'm not an expert in anything except making mistakes, but I do have a Ph.D. from the school of hard knocks and I'm a road scholar. America is my research lab, and I'm just a student of human nature." How could you not love that!

You'll need to surround yourself with a supporting cast that helps you remember your new lines. For the most part, people are afraid to disqualify gloomy dialogues and don't do it because they sense that the majority wants to have their negativity validated. But a really good friendship allows for honesty—not the kind that's hurtful or self-serving, but the straightforwardness that offers empathetic advice from a loving place.

I don't want everyone around me to agree with everything I do or say—and neither should you. You need to be called on your crazy stuff; otherwise, it will start to take on a life of its own and there won't be room for anyone else. Let me give you a small example of how capabilities, dreams, and desires are reduced. How many times have you told someone that your memory is shot? First of all, if "it's shot," then you don't have a whole lot of options. You've created quite a serious metaphor. I'm very visual, so I'm seeing a big hole in your head where your memory used to be stored. How do you repair it? Are you a surgeon? I guess you have to try to work around what's left, and that doesn't feel promising.

The facts are that memory can be compromised by stress, illness, medications, fatigue, and age. But in every instance, unless there has been severe damage, the brain can repair itself by creating new pathways. Your mind is able to store millions of bits of information, and like a computer that isn't being used, it will often place some data into long-term storage. It's also like riding a bicycle: When you practice using it, you become more proficient at it. So here's what you want to say when you don't have instant recall: "My memory is taking a quick nap but will be back very soon."

It's also a good idea to check in with someone who knows you well whom you can trust: a sort of "thought detective" when you say things that may not serve your best interests. An individual who's near and dear to you will know if your memory is going, so ask him or her to conduct a full investigation.

Here are some common statements that keep you limited, withered, and stuck in the black hole; they're followed (in italics) by my irreverent comebacks.

Ways to Wither

- I always get the slow line. *Well, I guess you're destined to grow old in line.*
- It's going to be a long day. *Huh, I thought most days contained the same amount of time.*
- I only have two hands. *Isn't that interesting!*

- You never listen to me. *Why should I?*
- I'm only one person. *Funny, I could have sworn you were a twin.*
- I'm the only one who gets anything done around here. *Maybe that's because you never trust anyone else enough to ask for help, and if you did, you wouldn't accept how they did it.*
- I'm getting sick over this. *Well, good for you. Now maybe you'll get a rest.*
- My life is a mess. *Maybe you need to clean it up.*
- I wish they'd treat me better. *I wish they would, too, but they won't until you do it first.*

Here are some statements that reek of personal empowerment, strength, and fun:

- *Today I remember everything that I need to know.*
- *When I think that my life is a mess, I buy a new broom and go to work.*
- *Everyone I meet treats me the way I treat myself, so I better treat myself well.*
- *I ask for help when I need it, instead of acting helpless.*

- *People listen to me because I have something to say.*
- *My mental, physical, and spiritual health is my responsibility.*

It's also a good idea to become aware of how often you use withered words that make life seem arid and devoid of succulence. The following are some examples that need to be extricated from your vocabulary because you could be at risk for dehydration.

Withered Words

shriveled	awful	wrinkled
desiccated	gnarled	cranky
"pruny"	nasty	wasted
miserable	pitiful	decrepit
hopeless	senile	stupid
pathetic	horrible	dumb

Now here are some luscious words that could make your life spurt.

Juicy Words

exuberance	charismatic	desirable
flourishing	magnificent	hearty
flaunt	divine	fortunate
flossy	delicious	flamboyant
juicy	alluring	flush
moist	ardent	flounce
succulent	astronomical	endear
dewy	decadent	vibrate
amazing	delightful	sumptuous
brilliant	dazzling	remarkable

Try describing yourself, your day, week, or life with some of these juicy words, in phrases like these:

- *I awake each morning feeling moist with life, and I create a magnificent day filled with divine people and amazing activities.*
- *I delight everyone who knows me with my brilliance and good fortune.*
- *My body and mind are juicy and delicious.*
- *I am filled with exuberance!*
- *My life is a dazzling array of remarkable happenings.*
- *My brain flourishes with succulent thoughts.*

I realize that what I'm advocating isn't a simple shift from ordinary language to a little over the top. I'm recommending *way* over the top because that might get you to the center. Why not give it a try? It's definitely not easy since you're accustomed to using a predictable vocabulary in everyday life, which relies on familiar, safe thoughts. But that doesn't create new and exciting outcomes—it just generates the same old results.

Trust me! This isn't merely an exercise to make you appear foolish or outrageous; instead, it will not only beef up your emotional responses but will also increase your brainpower. As you age, continually challenge and engage yourself in new ways of being. Remember that you're a veritable storehouse of thoughts, running 24 hours a day. *You have the choice to use them or lose them.* Isn't that marvelous?

Chapter 6

Walk on the Wild Side

"The important thing is not to stop questioning.
Curiosity has its own reason for existing.
One cannot help but be in awe when he contemplates
the mysteries of eternity, of life, of the marvelous
structure of reality. It is enough if one tries merely to
comprehend a little of this mystery every day.
Never lose a holy curiosity."
— Albert Einstein

One of my dear friends is Dr. John J. Ratey, the co-author of *Driven to Distraction* and a psychiatrist who specializes in attention deficit disorder (ADD). His mind is amazing, and I've been blessed to have many conversations with him about exciting topics. When we get together, time flies, and each subject we discuss makes me feel totally exhilarated. I have a great passion for neuroscience, and John's knowledge in this area is brilliant. What

I find most interesting is that in those moments, I feel incredible exuberance.

Serendipitously, John asked if I'd read the book *Exuberance,* by Kay Redfield Jamison. Since I hadn't, he sent me a copy and I was enthralled by its content. I felt validated at last but had to admit that this wasn't my first experience with this emotion. I'd been aware of its presence since childhood, and I knew that I possessed it far beyond many around me. My entire family—except for my grandmother Francesca, the martyr—embodies exuberance. It was hard to get away with unemotional responses. You never could just *like* something; you had to drool over it and use effusive language. We didn't know it, but we were trying to create contagious excitement.

When I'm onstage, my energy is transmitted to my audience. I see it happening, and I know that when I'm in the zone, I can create a little bit of pandemonium among those listening. I felt its force when I was in Montreal touring with President Clinton and Lance Armstrong. Eight thousand people got to their feet as I finished and started whooping and hollering like crazy—the result of my exuberance.

These joyful emotions are most obvious in children who have no limits to their enthusiasm, yet many grown-ups leave this powerful expression behind and have little or none left as they age. It's unfortunate that adults aren't given prizes for being excited about something. Most often it's the opposite: You're told to "Stop it!" and "Control yourself!" so you don't become too besotted with delight and pleasure over what you're doing or saying.

I believe that staying in touch with exuberance is an absolutely necessary part of aging. The question is how to do it. The responsibilities of life get in the way and it's easy to behave like an "Adult," but if you act too adult, you'll become *a dolt*—boring, unappealing, and difficult to be around. I'd like to propose some of the following succulent qualities for your consideration in order to refill your exuberance compartment.

Juicy Tidbits

Curiosity. There's no more permanent or certain characteristic of a vigorous mind than an unquenchable curiosity. I'm thankful that my grandparents never quelled my need to explore and seek out answers for many, many things. Children are born with incredible inquisitiveness—touching, smelling, and staring for long periods of time as they try to figure things out. Who hasn't had a child or been around one who continually asks "Why?"; and when it's answered, another why replaces it. The adult inevitably becomes exhausted and finally exclaims, "Because I said so!" . . . which only creates another why. Kids are like the Energizer Bunny in all its glory—they're a miniature FedEx. Nothing stops them!

Along the way, the desire to know may be dampened by overbearing parents or a life that has taken its toll on your spirit, but curiosity can be recaptured or enhanced by doing a variety of things. It really is about engaging and exploring. Try a few of my suggestions: Some ideas are simply being present wherever you are, and some require a bit of effort. You choose where you'd like to begin.

- Whenever you're in a place where you have to wait, engage others in conversation. Find out where they're from and what they do. I love talking to people because I find out a lot about how folks live, what types of things they do, and what part of the world they're from. I often hire limo drivers to pick me up at various airports and take me to my hotel. I've met some of the most fascinating individuals and gotten amazing information about the countries they come from. Now I also realize that not everyone wants to converse, so I use my intuition—I think most do like to chat, though.

- When you take a walk, notice what's around you—the foliage, the animals, the houses. Don't just look, examine deeply. I love to pick up a leaf and study its construction. Take nothing for granted! Imagine that little kid inside who would have asked why the leaf fell off the tree.

- Be available to others' inquisitiveness, whether it's coming from your children, grandchildren, mate, or co-worker. Don't stifle someone's need to know by using withered language such as "Oh, for goodness' sake, it's just a leaf. Get over it!"

If there ever were a trait that must be kept alive and constantly exercised, it's curiosity. It infuses the spirit that keeps us young.

Still Kickin'

Why We Love Lily Tomlin

From the time we first saw her back in 1969 on the revolutionary sketch comedy show *Rowan & Martin's Laugh-In,* we were amazed by the talent of Lily Tomlin. Her ability to create hilarious, memorable characters, such as Ernestine, the telephone operator ("Have I reached the party to whom I am speaking?"); and the confused five-year-old Edith Ann ("And that's the truth!") went way beyond the norms of comedy in those days. Indeed, those characters remain part of our popular culture today, almost 40 years later.

I love the fact that in the mid-'70s, AT&T offered Lily $500,000 to play Ernestine in a television commercial for the company—and she turned them down, knowing that such an appearance would hurt her integrity. But she wasn't shy! Soon afterward, Lily portrayed Ernestine in a mock-TV commercial during a *Saturday Night Live* skit, in which she famously tells the audience: "We don't care. We don't have to. We're the Phone Company."

But the comedienne can't be pigeonholed: She also broke our hearts in Robert Altman's film *Nashville,* in which she played the mother of deaf children. And in the 1990s, she surprised us as the tough-as-nails boss lady on the series *Murphy Brown.*

Her one-woman show *The Search for Signs of Intelligent Life in the Universe* is a once-in-a-lifetime mix of comedy, social satire, and wisdom about women's issues in the late 20th century. Incredibly, when she brought it back to Broadway in 2000 (at age 61), she could still command the stage for the full two hours, portraying a dozen characters in a demanding act of physicality and stamina. (One of the personalities is a 20-something teacher of an aerobics class—and Lily performs the segment in total exercise mode.)

And as she gets further into her 60s, she continues to amaze us with her ability to create complex and lovable characters—notably the eccentric and strong-willed Deborah Fiderer, who is the President's secretary, on the popular TV series *The West Wing*.

For her brilliance and integrity, we kick up our heels to Lily Tomlin.

Awe. I find it an incredible travesty that we're losing our sense of awe as a culture. Because of the plethora of products, foods, and entertainment, society has become somewhat jaded to the ordinary. I'm very concerned about today's young people and whether they'll be capable of living a long, healthy, juicy life. It seems that no matter what new gadget comes out, in no time at all it becomes a thing of the past.

Even at 86, my grandfather still had a twinkle in his eye whenever it was time to plan something—either a visit to someone's house, a meal, or an errand. It was never "Oh, I just did that last week" or "Why do we have to do that?" He immediately kicked into *Andiamo!* ("Let's go!") and never tired of anything except of course an illness or a tragedy. Then he'd throw his arms up and declare that it was now in God's hands.

If you have small children around, you'll notice that they have similar response mechanisms. Even if they see the same bug a hundred times, they're still captivated by it; whereas most adults are ready to squash it because it may bite. Jon Kabat-Zinn speaks to this beginners' mind in his book *Wherever You Go There You Are,* and points out that individuals must not lose the ability to see newness in everything, even if it has been looked over again and again. There's still room for awe—one can never discover the entirety of anything. As such, make becoming jaded your worst nightmare.

Spontaneity. How often do you do something just for the heck of it? There's no specific plan, no dire need—you do it *just because.* As time passes, it's easy to get into a rut and become a slave to a set way of being. It's like a yoke around your neck that's dragged around by a master you could refuse to obey but feel indebted to because it's safe and familiar. How dull to have lost the ability to just decide in the moment that you can do something different.

I realize that all of us have responsibilities, but we also have many life situations that aren't as serious as leaving a patient unsutured on the operating table. I'll never forget the Thanksgiving when I was about 13 years old. Everyone attended except one of my uncles who lived in Virginia. We were sitting at the table enjoying the meal when out of the blue my mother wondered aloud what my uncle might be doing. My cousin said we should call him. All of a sudden—and without much discussion—we piled into cars (turkey intact) and drove straight to my uncle's house. We didn't get there until midnight! They were sleeping, so we threw pebbles at the windows and they got up and finished dinner with us. It was totally off the wall . . . and unforgettable.

Our memories should be woven with unique and wonderful experiences. In the end, it's not how often we took a walk around the block that will bring a smile to our lips, it's the day we tried doing it backward. *Spontaneity is the surprise that our souls desire.* I can't suggest any activities because it would defeat the purpose! Premeditated spontaneity isn't living in the moment. So the ball is in your court.

Fantasy. I've been a great advocate of fantasy since I was a little girl. I was fortunate to live close to New York City; and my mother often took me to see Broadway plays, visit museums, or go to the opera. I also spent a lot of time watching old black-and-white movies, which is beginning to feel like I came from prehistoric days. In addition, I started dancing at a very young age. All of these activities enabled me to become extraordinarily adept at amusing myself.

Thank God I was blessed with this gift, because it has seen me through good and bad times. I've used it to get through simple activities such as waiting in line or sitting in a doctor's office for an appointment. Suddenly I'm caught up in being a dancer in Chicago or a jazz singer. When I'm stuck in an airport, I've often entertained myself by pretending that what's going on around me is part of a movie. And sexual fantasies are great whether you have a partner or not. You can choose anyone you want to have your virtual encounter with. It's all in your head, so no one can see or tell . . . or say they have a headache.

As you age, fantasies can come in handy and be entertaining if you let them. However, make sure you're not creating scenarios that feel anxious or sad. Unfortunately, some individuals are masters at that.

Surprise. I love surprises, and I really enjoy surprising others, too. It's one of those treasures in life that should never be abandoned. To really catch someone unexpectedly, you need to be awake and sensitive to what they say and do when they're with you.

"Waking up" is a continuous process. There's no limit to your awareness, but it takes practice. The poet Kabir expresses this idea very well: "If you are in a deep sleep, why waste time smoothing the bed and arranging the pillows?" It takes the ability to listen and be fully present in conversation so you're able to recall the things that please others. It doesn't have to be extravagant or complicated; in fact, it's the insignificant details that truly delight people. To remember how certain individuals take their coffee or what their favorite colors are means that you care and you've paid attention—you're awake!

Similarly, you need to remain open to the surprises that occur in your life. They can be lovely gestures from others, and sometimes they'll be nothing more than a sudden appreciation of something new and wonderful.

There's a profound side effect to living a life full of surprise: It can spur your ability to be grateful. To act as if each day has wonderful unknown opportunities opens the door to being thankful and feeling happiness. I've watched so many children clap their hands gleefully at a butterfly, flower, or rainbow—it's the merry delight in the unexpected that they're experiencing.

Fill your life with surprise and don't allow cynicism to become your ally, for it will only age you more quickly . . . then the only surprise you'll get is an early death.

Still Kickin'

Why We Love Betsey Johnson

Take a look in any Betsey Johnson retail store (there are dozens of them across the country and in major cities around the world), and you'll know right away why I love her.

Her clothing is full of humor and whimsy; and it's beautiful with a light touch that says vigor, brightness, and fun. Her designs are sexy, playful, innovative, and unique—just like Betsey herself.

What's amazing is that she's been doing things her way for more than 40 years. She's been a force in fashion since the '60s, when she was a part of the Warhol scene and Edie Sedgwick was one of her models. While the majority of fashion retailers are part of big corporate conglomerates, and most designers sell their retail stores within days of financial success, Betsey has stayed fiercely independent and wildly successful.

A survivor of breast cancer, she's now an advocate and helps raise awareness about the disease. However, when she was first diagnosed, she wanted to keep it a secret from everyone except her daughter. But very soon she realized that keeping anything bottled up just wasn't her style, and she could do a lot more good for the world by sharing her experience and using her fame to put the spotlight on breast cancer. She has created several original designs and has donated the proceeds to fight the disease. She has also made numerous appearances at fund-raising events.

Now in her 60s, Betsey shows no sign of slowing down, but she does sit back and enjoy life more often. Once a month she visits her vacation home in Mexico, which she calls Villa Betsey (not to be confused with Betseyville, a small hotel she renovated and rents to the public). And while she works from there, she spends at least a couple hours a day just having fun and taking in the warm and rejuvenating rays of the Mexican sun.

For doing cartwheels down the runway at the end of her seasonal fashion shows, for her advocacy, and for her exuberance and smarts and one-of-a-kind adventurousness, we kick up our heels in admiration to Betsey.

Chapter 7

If the Shoe Fits, Wear It

"Your only obligation in any lifetime is to be true to yourself."
— Richard Bach

Being true to oneself can be very difficult, especially for women. Society gives men permission to follow their bliss when it comes to work, play, and rest. I realize that some of this has evolved with the times, but a boundary exists that many women haven't yet crossed—and may not until they get a little older. They still feel the need to nurture everything they come into contact with, often at the expense of their health.

I find it interesting that June Cleaver seems to have returned from the dead. So many young women are repeating a history that I've long left behind. They work; take care of their homes; and enroll their children in sports, accelerated-learning classes, music lessons, and God knows what else so the little ones can graduate from kindergarten with high honors. These moms drive their children to and from all these numerous events in their big SUVs, while complaining how tired they are (or they spend hours on the phone deciding whose turn it is to carpool). If that's not enough, add in going to the gym, trying to make their home resemble a page out of *Martha Stewart Living*, and being sexy when it's expected.

The book *The Myth of the Perfect Mother* came out a couple of years ago, and it blew me away. I think someone must have cloned women from the '50s without the bouffant hairdos. . . . Many of today's young women are suffering from anxiety and depression. Gee, I can't imagine why.

I spent years believing that no one could do anything without my direction, and whatever needed to be taken care of would be done best by me. Age has not only tempered this for me, but also for many of my female friends who've realized that no one's going to reminisce about how they always left the kitchen sink spotless before they went to sleep at night. And they know they won't be celebrated for having made their bed every morning—better to be remembered for designing a dress out of the sheets!

When I was first married back in the Ice Age, I lived in Levittown, Long Island. I had a child immediately and was a wife/mother/homemaker extraordinaire. I used to clean my oven dials with Q-tips. One of my favorite respites during the day was to take a few minutes—because that's all I thought I could manage—to read Erma Bombeck's column in *Newsday.* She really had a handle on things.

Serendipitously, I was asked to be a keynote speaker at one of the first Erma Bombeck Writers' Workshops in her hometown of Dayton, Ohio. To me, Erma is the grand pooh-bah of being able to write about the absurdity of life without making it crass, mean, or sarcastic. She was one of a kind and a master at seeing the humor in women's daily activities.

When I look back on how obsessed I was with finding dirt and straightening up, I realize that it was merely a way to hide from myself. Marriage and children should have been the last things on my list at 19, but when people don't feel good about themselves and don't understand why, they mask it with a lot of distractions. I thought I was saving myself by leaving behind my childhood home life and the daily dysfunction that came with it, but little did I know that I brought it with me everywhere I went.

"Be who you are and say what you feel,
because those who matter don't mind,
and those who mind don't matter."
— Dr. Seuss

One of my favorite characters in *Alice's Adventures in Wonderland* is the caterpillar who sits on the mushroom and asks Alice: "Who are you?" I don't think many of us ask ourselves that until we get older. We're so busy doing our thing that it never occurs to us that it might not be *our* thing, but someone else's idea of what we should be doing. Hopefully, as we age our voice becomes more and more empowered, and we can learn to dismiss the obnoxious roommates who attempt to take residence in our heads.

Studies in adolescent female behavior show that self-esteem starts to decline during puberty. It can sometimes take a lifetime to understand how we went from victors to victims. Many of my women friends have found—or are finding—themselves in this predicament. Some have husbands who are ready to retire or have already done so, some have divorced, and others have never married and are now living alone or in a partnership with the gender of their choice.

The males of my generation were brought up to embody the role of the hunter: They went out to provide the family with what it needed: food, shelter, and clothing. We, the women, were told to continue gathering and nurturing, but along the way, females began to be defined by additional roles. On top of our normal duties, we were also expected to hunt. Many of my peers, including myself, have held down jobs while also taking care of the domestic front.

It wasn't an easy transition. It created a lot of confusion among the males, and it also led to less caretaking for the whole family. I personally found it extremely difficult to try to earn a living and then come home to cook, clean, be a mother and wife, and still have time for myself. I often went to bed feeling like an indentured servant, yearning to be freed.

My ex-husband had a very hard time with my increasing need to assert myself. Both of us were ill prepared to cope with a woman who was becoming more and more aware of her power, and also becoming more of a public figure.

Still Kickin'

Why We Love Eve Ensler

When Eve Ensler began performing *The Vagina Monologues* in the mid-1990s (when she was already in her 40s), newspapers in the United States wouldn't even run ads for the provocative one-woman show unless the title was somehow masked.

Her wild and moving play—which began with her alone, sitting on a stool and reading off note cards—has developed into an international phenomenon performed by amazingly diverse and talented women such as Glenn

Close, Jane Fonda, Whoopi Goldberg, Winona Ryder, and Alanis Morissette.

In Eve's world, Valentine's Day has been transformed into "V-Day," a time to celebrate all females and demand an end to violence against women. Founded in 1998 and now a powerful movement, V-Day (the V stands for Victory, Valentine, and Vagina) supports antiviolence groups across the globe and organizes benefit performances of *The Vagina Monologues* in theaters and college campuses worldwide, raising public awareness and millions of dollars to support causes that work to stop atrocities committed against women and girls. It has made Eve a global ambassador for feminism, and she continues to use her skills as a playwright to highlight injustice and brutality.

For being an artist who trusts her gut—and other body parts—to speak truths that women have known and were ready to hear out loud, for celebrating the female form even when it's less than perfect, and for never resting until the world is safe for all women and girls . . . we kick up our heels to Eve Ensler.

We're in the midst of a huge societal shift regarding the roles of marriage and family, and while the boomers have helped create it, they now must deal with the consequences. Many women no longer need a man to support them so they can be the little woman at home, yet we still have the instinctual need to be protected and cared for by a significant other. I believe that our biology struggles with the "new feminine models" every day.

I've had many a sleepless night over this conundrum. Having been born before the baby boom, I'm particularly susceptible to trying to make sense of everything that I was brought up to believe about who I *should* be. I began as a wife, mother, friend, cook, domestic engineer, gardener, chauffeur to three children, and occasional artist; and I've since added caretaker to my mother, lecturer, TV personality, writer, fund-raiser, and grandmother to 11. "Who am I?" is a very interesting question! I'm all those things, but now I understand that I don't have to be perfect at all of them. To be true to myself, I need to focus my energy on what I love most, and not be concerned about how the cans are lined up in the pantry.

Take the time to examine who you are—you deserve it. Write a short paragraph that describes your life and how you feel about it. Start off by asking yourself these questions:

- Who were you a decade ago?
- What were you doing?
- Can you recall how you felt about yourself?

- What are you doing now?
- Do you feel more or less authentic than you did years ago?
- What has changed?
- Is there anything that you want to do to improve, change, or increase your ability to become your most extraordinary self?

꩜ ꩜ ꩜

When menopause hits, it really starts to rock the boat. In *The Wisdom of Menopause,* my good friend Dr. Christiane Northrup has written extensively about the massive changes that occur during this time in a woman's life. It's as if the mind/body decides to give us a chance to reevaluate our situations by keeping us awake for hours so we can think about every stinkin' thing we've ever done and the consequences, both good and bad. And if that doesn't do it, then the hot flashes will. I consider it puberty in reverse. We often find ourselves vacillating between being Twisted Sister and the Fairy Godmother. It has a huge effect on women who have a lot of unresolved issues, especially childhood traumas.

This period in my life, or lack of (pun intended), was the beginning of a significant shift. For the first time, I began to acknowledge that my sense of humor had not only served me well in my career and life, but it had also shielded me from traumatic memories. I had buried my pain and had worn masks through the years, but now the fire of menopause was burning them off. It was a fiery storm that would continue until all of my façades were gone.

Storms often start in subtle ways, and mine began showing up in the many confrontations that my ex-husband and I would have about who should do what. Years of being a martyr and perfectionist became tiresome for me. We both wanted to be nurtured, but we had neither the skills nor the energy to express our needs.

The French existentialist writer Jean-Paul Sartre said, "Hell is other people," but this is only true when "hell" is the message we transmit. If our inner world is in chaos—a turbulent mass of anxieties, fears, and emotional baggage—it's easy to blame our problems and stress on others. We spend many hours of our lives blaming other people. If only we could recognize how little it benefits us, but nothing can change until we coax ourselves into awareness and wake up from our dysfunctional pasts.

Women of my generation have had great difficulty owning their power. I've been fascinated to read how actresses Ellen Burstyn and Jane Fonda spent years dissociated from their true selves in order to please the men in their lives so they could get what they thought they needed. We always saw their inner power just as many people saw mine, but Ellen and Jane couldn't detect it in themselves—and neither could I. That's the ultimate irony that many women have lived but are trying to relearn as they age.

We also now know that male and female brains are very different. We need some type of a gender-communication program so that both parties can understand what the other one is trying to say. Today's males are much more accustomed to women being multifaceted, but that doesn't mean the tug of war has gone away.

I also realized that as I unraveled the mysteries of my childhood and began owning the resulting feelings that rose to the surface, more than anything in the world I wanted to be me. I wish I could have been my true self in the context of my marriage, but the anger went on too long and was too hurtful. So here I am—along with lots of other women over the age of 50—coming to grips with the fallout from finally becoming my authentic self.

The following excerpt from the book *Eccentrics,* by Dr. David Weeks and Jamie James, is a perfect example of what I'm talking about. An artist named Anita describes the frustration and double standards she endures in her work:

> When a male artist says he wants to shut himself off and create, they say he's serious about his

> work. When I do it, I'm either being selfish or I have a psychological problem.
>
> I really shocked one woman when I told her I didn't want to have children. She got angry, and said that she had two lovely daughters and wouldn't trade them for the world. She stewed for a long time, and then she said she had me figured out—my creations were my "children." Can you believe that? How would she like it if I told her that she had children to make up for the fact that she couldn't draw?

What's unfortunate is that it's often *women* who find fault with or are critical of other women who wish to follow the road less traveled. I've found this to be true of mothers and grandmothers who spend every waking minute discussing, visiting, or showing off pictures of their offspring. And if you only have a few photos, you're perceived as heartless and part of the evil empire. We need to stop judging and spend more time validating each other and encouraging one another to take risks and live our lives boldly and fully.

Sadly, there also seems to be tension between women who stay home with their children and those who don't. The ones who don't work may be viewed as lesser people than the women who have jobs, and working moms may be considered selfish by stay-at-home moms. My mother worked and told me to make sure that I always had some mad money in case I needed to run away. However, she was the ultimate dichotomy: a brilliant legal stenographer who worked on Wall Street and who also rushed home every night and made dinner while still wearing her suit, as my stepfather relaxed and read the paper, periodically asking if dinner was ready.

My mother's rage was palpable, and now my heart goes out to her because I realize that she was deeply unfulfilled. She never discouraged me from having a career, although she wasn't too keen on what I chose. She really wanted me to be a schoolteacher so I'd have the summers off and a pension. To this day, she occasionally asks if I'm still flying around trying to make people laugh.

I found the years from 55 to 60 filled with a great deal of divergent emotions. My career was taking off, my second marriage was failing, my children were trying to figure out what to make of me, grandchildren were being born, and my mother was becoming increasingly more frail.

Role models for this stage in life aren't very visible in our society. Oh yes, we see older actresses who have maintained themselves at high levels so they can stay employed, but few are seen visiting their moms at a nursing home or being wheeled out of the hospital after a hip replacement. The reality is that the boomers, and those of us who are slightly before them (preboomers), are defining aging in new and exciting ways. Unfortunately, the media doesn't choose to focus on our lives as much as they do on the likes of Paris Hilton and on the marriages, divorces, and births of the Hollywood glitterati.

You can't stop the inevitable, but you can reinvent yourself in many ways. You can decide to live the life you dreamed of but thought was impossible because of self-imposed limitations or those placed upon you by parents, friends, or significant others.

I heard Wayne Dyer (who's in his 60s) tell someone that retirement should be your last breath. In fact, a centenarian study proves this: Many content and healthy individuals in their late 90s, and some who are 100, still go to work or regularly do something they're passionate about.

You can begin to emulate this behavior, too. I'm going to share my recipe for reinvention, which holds true no matter how old you are.

Juicy Tidbits

- Be aware of how you feel about your life. None of us are in a state of hysterical euphoria every day, but if in your day-to-day existence you sense an unease that doesn't go away, chances are it isn't indigestion.

- Open yourself to opportunities that come your way—listen, observe, and notice. Sometimes a friend or family member can be a conduit to something new that you might consider trying.

- Have a response ready. When someone asks what you're going to do with the rest of your life, tell them that you don't know, because at any given moment, whatever you're doing could be replaced with something you like even more. In other words, keep them guessing—explaining gets tiring, and they probably won't get it anyway.

- Study trends. Ken Dychtwald, Ph.D., has written several books on aging trends and has many great ideas to tap into if you need encouragement.

- Take classes online or at a university in what you long to do. There are currently individuals who are getting degrees in their 50s, 60s, 70s, and beyond.

- Allow yourself to believe that your mind is an immense playground you can access in order to discover what makes you happy.

- Find what you're passionate about and become who you were meant to be. It's not only healthy, but will prevent you from becoming a nag to others who are already doing what they love.

- Try it out. Check out **www.vocation-vacations.com** or **www.grownupcamps.com** for ideas about what you think you might want to do. You can spend a couple of days with someone to experience a vocation you've always dreamed about or stay at a weeklong camp for a variety of things you've fantasized about, such as being in a circus or singing in a rock-and-roll band.

- Get into therapy or find a coach. Look for someone who can help you make peace with the past; reframe some of your thinking, if necessary; and guide you toward a new, exciting future.

Above all, don't waste another minute discussing what doesn't work in your life or your fears about aging. *Do something about it!* Try the following visualization to spur you on:

Sit comfortably in a quiet place. Now close your eyes, breathe deeply for a few moments, and concentrate on simply being. Imagine yourself entering a beautiful room of your choosing. In the center, picture an ornate chest. Open it and gaze at its magical contents. The chest holds precious parts of your real self: your talents, virtues, dreams, passions, and generosity. Lovingly pick up each treasure and examine it. Think about what each one means to you and how it has served you. Know that they're always with you and can grow and continue to nurture you throughout your life. Open your eyes as you gently return. Think of these wonderful pieces of yourself whenever you forget who you truly are.

ၜ ၜ ၜ ၜ ၜ ၜ

Chapter 8

You Can't Kick Up Your Heels Unless Your Brain Is Working

"I am learning all the time.
The tombstone will be my diploma."
— Eartha Kitt

Keeping our minds agile is something we must continue to do throughout our lives. Neuroscientists are finding out more and more about the brain's amazing ability to adapt and reconfigure itself—not only when it's traumatized, but also as it ages. It was once thought that as we got older, our brains simply grew dimmer like a lightbulb on its last bit of wattage. But lo and behold, it's not so simplistic. Research now indicates that as the brain ages, it begins making connections and cross-indexing in ways it never has before.

Our short-term memory may not have the power it once had, and it may be harder to cram in a lot of raw information, but the minds of older folks have the ability to make associations and infer meanings that are beyond the capacity of younger minds. For many of us, the aging process actually makes the brain work better.

How we take care of our bodies is a big piece of the pie (and too much pie can be a huge problem). At this point, I think we're all aware of the fact that spending half of our lives on the sofa with the remote control in hand while eating a pile of french fries and onion rings isn't going to help our brains become juicy. We have to *move* in order to get enough oxygen to the brain so that we can think clearly.

The brain also needs the stimulation of positive emotions, learning experiences, and new ways of *being* to keep it young and fresh; and it requires love and support from other humans. We want to increase neuroplasticity, the lifeblood of our brains' ability to stay vibrant and alive. There are many ways in which we can embark on this exciting journey to build our minds' capabilities, so let's explore some of them.

A Love of Learning

It's difficult to think of a person who doesn't have the desire to learn—whether the subject is history, sports, politics, cooking, or just plain trivia. In an article by Ben Dean, Ph.D., he shows the scientific evidence that links a love of learning to longevity and good health: "Some researchers speculate that an across-the-board absence of [the desire to learn] may be indicative of pathology (Peterson and Seligman, 2004; Travers, 1978). . . . [And] research suggests that individuals who are able to develop and maintain interests later in life are likely to be more physically and mentally healthy than their less-engaged peers (Krapp & Lewalter, 2001; Renninger & Shumar, 2002; Snowdon, 2001)."

There has been incredible validation by science in this area. What we learn and how we do it will greatly influence our future. I can still see my grandfather at 86 sitting at the table with his espresso, an Italian newspaper, and stacks of books close at hand. And my mother never stopped flaunting her latest findings about the stock market or something interesting she'd heard on *Larry King Live*. Every time we chatted, she'd start with, "Did you hear about . . ." or "Did you know. . . ." I felt compelled to keep up with her.

I do the same thing with my children and grandchildren because I want them to stay on top of things—not be pushed under by them. The grandkids know I won't put up with the common kid complaint: "I'm bored." I knew never to say that because I'd always get the same response: "Go read a book!" or "Go clean your room." My take is a little different because I'm a bit more irreverent than my mother. I told my grandkids that boredom is a sign of "inner stupidity," and if they felt they had a functioning brain, they'd never utter that phrase. Trust me—they don't say it anymore.

Having a juicy brain takes some effort. It doesn't happen by simply going through life as if we were on dial tone. As a nation, we're overly focused on what we look like, what we own, and how much money we have. What would happen if we made education a priority for everyone? Would it help the fight against the poverty, violence, and misery that permeate so much of the world—in addition to increasing and sharpening our brain function as we age?

If you'd like to have your memory checked, go to **www.nationalmemoryscreening.org** or call 866-AFA-8484 to find out where you can get a free screening.

The type of learning style that I love and hope that everyone becomes interested in is the multidisciplinary method. Many of us are taught to fit in and be one-track thinkers, but when we start to look at subject matters from different perspectives, we begin to engage the whole brain. By practicing and applying the powers of observation, concentration, imagination, and association, we strengthen and develop the right brain as well as the left; and if we integrate both sides, we become more creative.

Here's an example of what I'm talking about: If you're reading a book about the Russian Revolution and it really piques your interest, don't stop there. Check out the music and artwork that might have evolved during that tumultuous period. Dive deep and find out what kinds of food and wine people enjoyed then or the types of architecture and clothing that were popular. Could you take a trip there and see some of the sites firsthand? If you make a point of having conversations with people you meet in your everyday travels, you may even discover that you know someone of Russian descent. I've often gotten amazing insight into a variety of global cultures from the individuals I meet while traveling to and from my various seminars.

I recently saw an advertisement for an all-day conference that focused on lifelong learning and was promoted as a "health club for the mind." This is a phenomenon waiting to happen. The emergence of neuroscience as "sexy" has created and will inspire vast business opportunities for those who have an ear for what's happening in society.

Meanwhile, I'm certain that the rest of us want to ensure that our brains look as good as our toned arms and thighs; otherwise, what's the point? You might as well check in to Madame Tussauds.

Still Kickin'

Why We Love Glenn Close

From her edgy, crazed performance as the rejected lover in *Fatal Attraction,* to her decision to play a tough L.A. police captain in the television series *The Shield,* we've loved Glenn Close for the fierce feminine power she brings to the screen. And speaking of tenacious femininity, what other 50-something iconic actress could have celebrated her private parts with quite as much bravado as Glenn did while performing *The Vagina Monologues?*

She's pushing 60, is recently remarried, and swims 50 laps a day. She spends a great deal of her time working for charitable causes, including raising awareness of AIDS and offering help to its most powerless victims, shining the media spotlight on the plight of people suffering with breast and ovarian cancers, and showing the need to provide educational opportunities to women who are serving long-term prison sentences.

In every way, she's someone who takes the path less traveled, makes daring choices, and boldly follows her passions . . . while enlightening and entertaining all of us along the way.

Ways to Wither

- Give up trying to remember things, and don't attempt to learn anything new. Use the following statements to make yourself feel justified: "What's the use of learning new things? I can't remember them anyway" or "I'm sick of learning; I already know everything I'll ever need to know."
- Keep referring to the same information as if it were sacred. Don't allow anyone to persuade you to see how you might look at things differently.
- Refrain from using any new technology in case it forces you to have to relearn how to do something. And hold on to your Walkman until the Smithsonian calls because they want to add it to their collection.

Juicy Tidbits

- Buy the Nintendo DS Lite. It's a high-powered handheld video game system that you can easily take wherever you go. I bought it because it has some games that predominantly focus on increasing learning capabilities. *Brain Age* and *Big Brain*

Academy are educational games that were inspired by the work of the prominent Japanese neuroscientist Dr. Ryuta Kawashima.

- Place a dictionary on your nightstand. Study one word every night before bed, and then try to use it the next day during your conversations. My mother used to do this with me. Each evening at dinner, she'd ask me what new word I had learned, and then I'd have to use it in a sentence.

- Write down a list of up to ten words, and then try to recall them after about a minute. Now wait a few more minutes and go back and see how many you can remember. Try it again in an hour. Continue doing it to expand and exercise your memory.

- Keep your observational skills keen by walking into a room and scanning it as if you were a forensic scientist from the TV series *CSI*. Try to remember the placement of the furniture, the color of the walls, and any other distinguishing features. Make a game of it with friends when you're on an outing.

- Try exercising all of your senses. Listen carefully; look deeply; and think about how things feel, smell, and taste. Make your life an eclectic learning experience.

Visualization

I've found that one of the best ways to enhance memory is through the use of visualization. I've always had a very visual mind. A lot of the information in your long-term memory is visual, so your memory (as well as your ability to learn new skills) will greatly improve if you spend more time using this technique. Visualization is considered to be one of the most effective ways to jog your memory. These types of aids are also known as *mnemonics.*

You can use visualization in many areas of your life aside from exercising your memory. It can be an invaluable tool for healing, weight loss, relationship issues, insomnia, self-worth, addictions, and a host of other issues too numerous to mention. For more information and specific programs that will help you with the process, log on to **www.healthjourneys.com**. Belleruth Naparstek is the founder of this company and is a leading authority on guided imagery.

Try this exercise just for the fun of it:

Sit in your favorite chair and make yourself comfortable. Close your eyes and take a few minutes to just breathe deeply and fully.

Keep your eyes closed as you do the following: Imagine yourself holding an orange. Raise it to your nose and inhale its citrusy fragrance. See yourself cutting the orange, picking up one half of it, and gently sucking the juice out. Can you taste the flavor? Are you able to experience the sweetness of the orange and the texture of the pulp? What type of sensations are you feeling as the juice slides down your throat? Can you smell it in the air around you?

Now open your eyes. Sometime during the next few hours, try to recall the experience. Imagine all the possibilities and various images you can conjure up!

Meditation

Meditation differs from visualization in that it's geared to help remove the mind from its incessant need to make you feel crazed and humorless. I'm sure you're familiar with how easy it is to be continually distracted from the present moment by your internal critics, who are hell-bent on constantly reminding you of what you haven't completed or how inept you are at what you *are* doing.

Meditation isn't rocket science. You can start with a simple process:

Sit in a comfortable chair and position yourself so that you're completely relaxed and at ease. Then breathe in and out as you always do, but every time you exhale, say "Just breathing"; or instead, use a word that brings forth peaceful emotions, such as love or joy. You can also recite the beginning of a prayer. Try it for five minutes and then increase it to 15 minutes or longer. At first your mind will try to sabotage you, but let it do its thing. Address it by saying, "Just thinking," allowing the commotion to pass as you gently return to your breathing and words.

This takes practice, but the rewards could be lowered blood pressure, less anxiety, stronger immunity, more inner peace, and a sense that all is well with the world *right now.* After a while, your body/mind will integrate this calming meditative state to the degree that you can access it whenever you begin to make yourself nutty. *This should be a daily practice!*

A team of researchers headed by Sara Lazar, a research scientist at Massachusetts General Hospital, showed that the gray matter of the cerebral cortexes of 20 men and women who meditated for just 40 minutes a day was thicker than people who didn't meditate at all. These are the parts of the brain involved in attention and sensory processing. "The difference was especially notable in older volunteers, suggesting that meditation may help reduce the cortical thinning that comes with age," according to Lazar and her colleagues. Most studies of meditation have focused on Buddhist monks who practice meditation for several hours, but this research illustrates that you don't have to do it all day to get results. Who knows, we may eventually get to drive-through meditation.

Still Kickin'

Why We Love Clint Eastwood

Clint has always been a powerful screen presence, even before he uttered the iconic line: "Go ahead, make my day," as "Dirty" Harry Callahan. But his creative strengths as a director and composer are just as amazing. So many people complain about getting out of their chair in their 70s; and then there are the exceptions like Clint, who's still acting, directing, writing, and composing music for Oscar-caliber movies.

Even if he didn't look the way he does, how could you not love a man who's given us movies such as *Million Dollar Baby, Mystic River, The Unforgiven,* and *Flags of Our Fathers?*

And on top of his artistic mojo, he's a political force as well. He's a man who feels strongly about his community (he even served as the mayor of his town, Carmel, California, for a term—and made two movies at the same time) and like in most other ways, Clint is his own man in the political arena. He's registered as a Republican but supported Democratic governor Gray Davis, who was targeted for a recall.

Clint summed up his beliefs in a recent interview: "I don't see myself as conservative, but I'm not ultra-leftist. You build a philosophy of your own. I like the libertarian view, which is to leave everyone alone. Even as a kid, I was annoyed by people who wanted to tell everyone how to live."

For being someone who becomes more interesting every day and who dives into new projects with passion and enormous curiosity, we kick up our heels to Clint Eastwood.

Chapter 9

Sexual Heeling

"Love is the answer, but while you're waiting for the answer sex raises some pretty good questions."
— Woody Allen

There's nothing juicier than sex! However, it's often portrayed in movies or by the media as something that only the young are capable of performing. We're assaulted with images of half-dressed bodies selling everything from grapefruit to gum. The ads often reflect individuals with wet lips, lascivious looks in their eyes, and bodies that seem like they're devoid of excess flesh. Who can ever forget the sexual gymnastics in the movie *Basic Instinct?* At one point, the lovers are having sex in the sink while the female protagonist is ooh-ing and aahing to beat the band. Frankly, I think she was being stuck in the butt with some forks and knives that hadn't been put in the dishwasher.

Even in our youth, how many of us were actually capable of contorting ourselves into some of the positions people get into in order to have a sexual encounter? Why not just audition for Cirque du Soleil? Sex isn't simply about being a trapeze artist or going at it all day until the paramedics have to be called. It encompasses the mind, body, and spirit and can become a deeply intimate experience as we age if we take the time and make the effort.

Many partners become complacent and repeat the same routine over and over, thinking the outcome will be better than the last time. It's a lot like eating cornflakes every day and expecting them to taste like steak after a month or two goes by. The bottom line is that we must grow and change to keep lovemaking interesting.

A lot of women who once thought that satisfying a man was the primary function of having sex have matured into the realization that it isn't all about the men. How many of us have tried so hard to make our partners feel confident that we produced sounds resembling the famous scene in *When Harry Met Sally . . .*—when Sally fakes an orgasm in the restaurant to prove that it sounds authentic—only to realize later on that we cheated ourselves in order to feed someone else's ego? I hope that we've all made a pact with ourselves to never fake anything again. It only enhances the withering process.

Sometimes sexual inertia is created by our aging biology or the side effects of medications that we take for various conditions. Viagra has become a household name and a lifesaver for a lot of men who experience erectile dysfunction. It has possible side effects, but what doesn't? The latest, greatest prescription drug Cialis allows men to have a longer window of opportunity; however, the commercial always adds that if the user has an erection that lasts longer than 36 hours, he should go to the emergency room. My irreverent humor kicks in, and I can't help but think, *Why waste it? Maybe these guys can go outside and dig holes for spring bulbs, or use it as a pool skimmer.* You have to admit that this "member" that seems to have a life of its own is very funny.

I've spoken to some women who find this new zest for sex on the part of their mates to be tedious after a while. Even if dehydration sets in, too much water can become toxic.

The ultimate irony is that the couples portrayed in most of the ads don't look like they need any help. As in all commercials, everyone needs to look younger than the market they're appealing to. I recently saw an ad for Depend undergarments, and the model couldn't have been more than 30. Is this a new trend? Are bladders becoming older sooner? Of course not! It's because every product needs a youthful representative. It gives a very clear and dysfunctional message: As you age, you disappear.

Still Kickin'

Why We Love Marianne J. Legato, M.D.

Dr. Marianne Legato, now 72, is the daughter of a physician. Her earliest memories are of accompanying her father on his hospital rounds, which were the only occasions when she was able to spend time alone with him. Ironically, her father vehemently opposed her decision to follow him into medicine because he was of the old-school belief that a woman's first allegiance must be to her husband and family—and that didn't conform to the lifestyle of a doctor. Seeing her determination, her father offered to let her practice with him if she agreed never to marry. She refused, and they became estranged for decades.

Marianne has gone on to an extraordinary 40-year career in medicine and is on the forefront of studying how gender differences should be factored into medical practices. She has written several books, including the recent *Why Men Never Remember and Women Never Forget.* (I'd love her just for coming up with that title, if nothing else!)

In addition to being a practicing internist and a professor of medicine at the prestigious Columbia University, this strong, independent woman travels extensively, lecturing in support of the science she so believes in. Marianne writes books, wins awards, and continues to have a major influence on the way that the medical community pays attention to the differences between men's and women's bodies. She's truly a force of nature.

All kidding aside, there's a very real issue about how aging affects sexuality. From her book *Why Men Never Remember and Women Never Forget,* Marianne J. Legato, M.D., FACP, highlights some statistics:

> A recent survey, put out by University of Chicago sociologist Edward Laumann, Ph.D. (and sponsored by Pfizer, the company that makes Viagra), showed that many older women may be coping with partners who suffer from sexual dysfunction. Of the nearly 28,000 men and women over the age of 40 in 30 countries who were surveyed, 20 percent of men over 40 said they suffered from erectile dysfunction. Dr. Laumann also found that men became sexually dysfunctional twice as quickly as women did as they aged.

Perhaps the abundant research in erectile dysfunction goes hand in hand with the fact that men seem to be biologically more interested in sex, and also need it to define their self-worth. It's been said that a man has an erotic thought every 60 seconds, whereas a woman has one maybe once or twice a day. As testosterone diminishes, males are apt to be more invested in intimacy and are usually more willing to reveal their vulnerability. This is why so many of them allow their emotions to come closer to the surface as they age. Some men find themselves crying more easily, and they also make attempts to develop closer bonds to their partners and family members. While this is a relief to many women who've been begging their other half to get in touch with their emotions, it also has a downside: As women age, they seek more freedom and less emotional responsibility. They seem to want to return to their preadolescent years when young girls were more likely to tune in to their authentic selves.

And what of the women? Our bodies change just as much as our male counterparts, yet there are fewer remedies. Someone's working on a female version of Viagra, but we're complex creatures and our juiciness often lies more in our heads and hearts than in our private parts. This goes to show that sexuality isn't just about genitals—it's a state of being and a chemistry that we elicit when we embrace our sexual energy and others acknowledge its existence.

When we share loving intimacy with someone, we release oxytocin, a hormone found in nursing mothers' milk. It promotes calmness and helps us connect to a person in the same way that a mother bonds with her baby. And yes, estrogen (as well as other hormones) is a vital component in a comfortable sexual experience and may play a role in having a healthy libido, too. As estrogen diminishes, the vagina becomes less moist and it may be harder to become physically aroused; however, I've talked to women who had begun a love affair in their later years and found that the well hadn't dried up. After years of sexual dormancy, their anatomy not only woke up, but rocked with desire—and this was without any help from hormone replacements.

A woman's self-image is also extremely important to her sexuality. Having a partner may certainly help enforce or increase feelings of being sexually desirable, but if that option isn't available, we still must work on elevating our sense of self and maintaining a sexual relationship with ourselves.

Haven't we all witnessed women and men who don't look like the standard sex symbols but who electrify a room with their presence? Is there a way to develop this without appearing to be a clone of Catherine Zeta-Jones or Brad Pitt? Society doesn't make it easy for us to age and remain sexy, especially for women. However, Europeans seem to accept and appreciate them as they do aged wines—younger men seem to be just as intrigued with sophisticated older women as they are with younger ones.

When I was in Deauville, France, many years ago, I was struck by the fact that there were many women of all ages who were topless and nearly bottomless strolling the boardwalk. I was quite young and was filled with critical judgments about their bodies; and I kept thinking that if I looked like some of those older ladies, I would have been wearing a shroud. Believe me, I get it now!

There are also a lot of younger men in committed relationships with older women, and we're just beginning to accept this reality. Perhaps we have Demi Moore to thank for this new, exciting trend. I still find it astounding that my great-grandmother decided to buck social mores by marrying a man 21 years her junior.

I tried a Website called **Agematch.com** for a while and was shocked by how many younger men e-mailed me. It was a real boost to my ego, but I didn't think that I was quite ready for a relationship. I needed to do a little more work on getting rid of my old inner critics, and I literally couldn't imagine myself butt naked with someone 20 years younger than I am. I looked in the mirror and saw a body that isn't bad, but according to those inner voices, it should be a lot better. Although if I wait too much longer, I'll be having my next romance graveside.

I know that this is my stuff and I have to work on it, but isn't it difficult to remove ourselves from the images of youthful-looking bodies that we're constantly bombarded with? The obsession with having perky, full breasts; butts that are so high they sit on shoulders; and abdomens that are so flat we can bounce quarters on them may be okay if we have the ability to spend most of our lives devoted to our bodies. But the idea that 50-, 60-, and 70-year-olds can imitate that look is usually ludicrous. It may be plausible for those individuals who've never deviated from their fitness regimen or for celebrities with the available income to hire a staff whose sole job is to be their drill sergeants.

Most of us are trying to hold down jobs, take care of family matters, and God knows what else; and besides all of that, nature does take its toll. We can lift body parts till the cows come home, but we still have to deal with the fact that our internal organs get old. We need plastic surgeons for the inside so that we can have a liver lift or liposuction on our brains.

I often wish we were back in the days when a Rubenesque figure was the type that men sought out. A rounded belly, ample thighs, and round and somewhat droopy breasts was once seen as the height of female perfection! It's unfortunate that most women today are so unhappy with themselves. More than 90 percent have poor body images, and they pass down those negative emotions to their children. Now men are starting to catch up, too.

You may be thinking that I'm giving you mixed messages. On the one hand, I'm advocating exercise and a healthy weight; however, I'm also stressing acceptance of your body. Believe it or not, the two can form a marriage that's very appealing and sexy. Strong individuals at the proper body weight, or with a little extra poundage, who embrace their aging bodies have a certain attitude called confidence that's extremely attractive. Self-confidence doesn't only emanate from chiseled shapes. I've met many physically beautiful people who have no sense of self-worth whatsoever.

How you feel about yourself as a sexual being also comes from the messages you've gotten from parents, peers, and past sexual experiences—both positive and negative. You can become severely compromised from sexual and emotional abuse. It's a difficult situation for men and women to revisit, but one that can be addressed through counseling or group support. If you've suffered through this kind of trauma, you owe it to yourself and your loved ones to get help. I know the pain of this from my own personal experience, and I'll discuss it in a subsequent chapter.

I don't know how invested men are in seeing themselves in an unflattering manner, but I do know that women are masters at it. I sincerely doubt that most guys bond by sharing negative information about themselves. Have you ever heard a group of men comparing how bloated they are or how awful their hair looks? Has any man ever shared with another the thought that his penis isn't quite as hefty as it once was? I'm pretty sure that's why they don't go to the men's room together. Females go in groups so we can share how awful we look and hope to hell that some other woman will try to win the contest.

How often do we focus on how good we look and how enticing we are? It's time we started to see ourselves as confident and attractive. We need to own our sexuality and honor it for the power it has to make us feel energetic, vital, and appealing.

Ways to Wither

- Never engage in sexual thoughts or fantasies. Behave as if you were preparing to move into a monastery.
- Act disgusted if friends share how wonderful they feel about their sexuality, and don't bother to find out why you feel that way.
- Pretend to enjoy sex. Fake orgasms and just please your partner since that's what you were taught to do.
- Use sex as leverage in your relationships.
- Make sure that your parts dry up and shrivel until nothing is left but a pile of dust.

Juicy Tidbits

- Schedule an extensive physical every year. Have your arteries checked for blood flow. Loss of libido isn't always the result of a diminishing interest in sex.

- Ask your physician to prescribe a vaginal estrogen treatment to keep things juicy. Guys should have their levels of testosterone checked. A reduction in hormones can cause fatigue, depression, and a decreased sex drive, but there are prescription patches available that you can apply to your skin to raise levels.

- Stick to a regular exercise program. It helps pump blood to all parts of your body—arousal needs blood flow.

- Try to maintain a healthy weight. It helps decrease your risks of hypertension, diabetes, heart disease, breathing problems, and joint pain. It's hard to roll around in the sack if you can't catch your breath and your joints are too rusty to move!

- Check all of your medications for side effects that might include sexual difficulties. Many antidepressants, blood-pressure medicines, and cardiac drugs come with these unfortunate effects, as well as many others. Don't stop taking them, but do examine your lifestyle. You may be able to take less medication if you take better care of yourself.

- Get lots of massages. It's a great way to get touched without having to do anything but lie there and enjoy yourself.

- Read the book *For Women Only: A Revolutionary Guide to Reclaiming Your Sex Life,* by Jennifer Berman, M.D., and Laura Berman, Ph.D. The Bermans are sisters who've picked up where Masters and Johnson left off. They have a clinic in Los Angeles and are incredibly savvy about women's sexuality.

- Watch some fun, sexy movies starring juicy older men and women. One of my favorites is *Shirley Valentine,* which tells the story of a married woman who sets off alone for an adventurous vacation in Greece. I think every woman should invite friends over and watch this—you'll love it!

- Be bolder. Flaunt yourself a little now and then, and act as if you're desirable and sexy. Who knows . . . at the very least, you'll amuse yourself!

ʚɞ ʚɞ ʚɞ ʚɞ ʚɞ ʚɞ

Chapter 10

Humor Your Heels

"In the end, everything is a gag."
— Charlie Chaplin

Nothing is as important as a sense of humor when it comes to aging well. Studies of centenarians have revealed that it's one of the three most vital coping mechanisms that healthy individuals possess; therefore, it's crucial to living a long, happy life.

I believe that the combination of my gene pool and the circumstances of my birth allowed me to have the awareness of the comedy and absurdity of life. See, I was a breech delivery, which means that I came out "ass-ways." It's given me a great appreciation of how asinine we can all be! My mother had a very hard labor; according to her, it went on for 40 days and 40 nights. She must have been on Noah's ark in a past life. I've heard the story hundreds of times, so I know that she suffered at length in order to bring me to this earthly paradise.

She also used her painful labor as an effective tool for inciting guilt when she wanted me to do something for her. Typically her comment would be, "If it wasn't for me and all the pain I went through, you wouldn't be here!" On top of that, I was told that I almost died. My mother gave birth to me at home with a doctor and her best friend, Josephine, in attendance. As the physician feverishly worked on my mother, he finally pulled me out and placed me on the bureau but then announced that I had already turned blue and might not make it. Josephine had other plans and began madly pounding my back while alternately clearing my throat.

The story goes that I didn't cry; instead, I smiled, closed my eyes, and went to sleep. I believe I had a near-death experience. I don't know about white lights and tunnels, but I do think that powerful moment stuck with me. You're too soon dead, so lighten up!

I've personally witnessed the importance of humor and aging. My 96-year-old mother amazes me with her funny remarks. She has difficulty hearing and seems to have trouble connecting all the dots, but she continually blurts out observations that crack me up—and she's still zinging people with her laser-sharp sarcasm.

In a recent visit, we had lunch with three other women who were in varying stages of dementia. Afterward as my mom, hunched over, pushed her walker down the hall, she turned to me and said, "Some of those women are on their third coffins." Although I'm very much in favor of empathetic humor over sarcasm, I still relish the fact that my mom is capable of laughing at life.

I've conducted hundreds of seminars for cancer patients, survivors, and their family members; and I've been awestruck by their incredible ability to laugh at what would make most of us shudder. My daughter, Laurie, was recently diagnosed with non-Hodgkin's lymphoma, and I can't begin to explain the shock I felt when I found out. She takes very good care of herself and even owns a Pilates studio. Halfway through the conversation in which Laurie told me about her diagnosis, she started laughing and said that she should have been a couch potato. Instead of all those years of veggies, fruits, and fish, she wished she had eaten lots of fries, burgers, and soda.

We all know that cancer doesn't choose its hosts based on people's health—or lack of it. Unfortunately, many individuals have died from this dreaded disease even though they were following a routine filled with nutritious foods and daily exercise. Yes, it's certainly a far better lifestyle for many reasons, but it doesn't guarantee life ever after.

Ironically, I've found that many of the people I've spoken to who are afflicted with cancer or other life-threatening illnesses have been amazingly invested in comedy. Called *gallows humor,* it supplies individuals with a coping mechanism and a way to deflect the stress they're experiencing. Remember the classic television series *M*A*S*H?* That was a perfect example of characters using this type of humor to overcome the horrors of war. The trials of aging remind me of that show. All of us will have to survive and somehow manage the traumas that are handed to us as we get older . . . and what better way to do it than with a sense of humor.

When I had my hip replaced, I went into the operation using my playfulness to ease the fear of going under the knife. Because I had previously held a workshop at that hospital, the nurses who prepped me were totally prepared for my banter and were ready to participate.

It was four days before Christmas, and they'd gotten funny hats to wear in my honor. They were all shocked by how low my blood pressure was just before surgery . . . but given the humorous situation and my outlook, it made sense. There's scientific literature that supports the fact that when people laugh, "feel good" chemicals rush forth with each giggle and help the body stay well. Now there's research that even shows that laughter can help prevent heart disease because it may actually expand capillaries.

Life is going to hand you lemons—there's no question about that. But instead of making lemonade, as the cliché goes, you may be better off just laughing about it.

Yes, finding comic relief in bad situations can be a lifesaver, but God knows, don't wait for a dismal diagnosis to get started. You have many opportunities to manifest humor in day-to-day life. I often feel as if I'm in the middle of a sitcom as I go through the day. My observational skills have always been my greatest asset, and they go into high gear whenever my radar senses absurdity.

For example, I've found myself laughing more at the TV commercials than during the actual shows I've been watching. I crack up over the ads for Lunesta, which feature a giant butterfly flapping its wings around the head of a woman sleeping peacefully. What's with that? If I ever saw that thing in my bedroom, I'd never sleep again!

And why does every little product these days have to be treated as if it's the result of decades of intense research? I went to buy a new mattress and was helped by a "sleep consultant" who was dressed not unlike an emergency-room physician. He then proceeded to walk me through a ten-page questionnaire to assess my sleep quotient. It felt more like preparation for a CAT scan than buying a bed, for God's sake—now that's funny!

If you think humor is too difficult to incorporate into your life, ease into it. *You have the ability to laugh.* Instead of becoming upset at those difficult and stressful moments, try to find a way to giggle at the ridiculousness of them.

Still Kickin'

Why We Love Bette Midler

Has there ever been a person who's redefined herself as many times, and tried as many different things, as Bette Midler has?

We first heard about her in the '70s when she took New York City by storm, singing and performing stand-up in gay bathhouses where she earned the nickname "the Divine Miss M." Bette's bawdy comedy, powerhouse voice, and voluptuous figure made her a cult celebrity; and she became a mainstream sensation when she took her act to Broadway in the *Clams on the Half Shell Revue.*

Soon afterward she tested her acting chops and received an Academy Award nomination playing a character based on the life of Janis Joplin in the drama *The Rose.*

In the late '80s, she embarked on the opposite path and began appearing in a string of comedic roles in feature films, such as the hilarious *Down and Out in Beverly Hills, Outrageous Fortune, Ruthless People,* and many others.

But all along, she continued to fuse her acting and voice talents by singing powerful dramatic ballads; her songs "Wind Beneath My Wings" and "From a Distance" were both

Grammy Award winners.

The girl who became famous for wearing clamshells on her breasts and telling raunchy Sophie Tucker jokes grew into a richly nuanced performer who's one of the most beloved stars in America.

She also uses her influence to help others. In 1995 she founded The New York Restoration Project, an organization that restores and beautifies parks in economically disadvantaged neighborhoods throughout the city—making it a better place to live for thousands of people who are in need of rejuvenating outdoor space.

For revitalizing our spirits *and* our landscapes . . . we kick up our heels to Bette!

I'd like you to take the following test to determine your humor quotient:

Humor-Quotient Test

Read the statements below and circle the number that best applies to you. If you circle a 7, you're agreeing wholeheartedly that the statement is *very characteristic* of you (in other words, you're saying, "I'm perfect and couldn't improve!"). If you circle a

1, the statement is *very uncharacteristic* of you ("Not me! I may need a 'humor transplant.'"). A 4 is when you're truly in the middle of the road, and the rest of the numbers are lesser degrees of a 1 and 7. Be honest—no one's watching!

1. My boss would describe me as a "Humor Asset" because my sense of humor benefits the company.

   7 6 5 4 3 2 1

2. My co-workers and family members consider my sense of humor one of my best traits.

   7 6 5 4 3 2 1

3. I avoid sarcasm, ethnic, or negative humor except in private conversations with close friends.

   7 6 5 4 3 2 1

4. I can laugh at my own mistakes and enjoy occasionally being poked fun at.

   7 6 5 4 3 2 1

5. I laugh alone when I feel that something is funny.

   7 6 5 4 3 2 1

6. As a humor consumer, I laugh easily and enjoy chuckling at jokes and stories that others share.

   7 6 5 4 3 2 1

7. I seek out cartoons, comedy shows, comedians, and other humor stimulants.

   7 6 5 4 3 2 1

8. I write down comical stories, and save cartoons and articles that make me laugh.

   7 6 5 4 3 2 1

9. When I'm stressed on the job, my sense of humor helps me keep my perspective.

   7 6 5 4 3 2 1

10. I spontaneously look for the funny side of life and share it with others.

    7 6 5 4 3 2 1

11. I send humorous notes and cartoons to friends, co-workers, and family members.

    7 6 5 4 3 2 1

12. My sense of humor makes it hard for people to stay mad at me.

    7 6 5 4 3 2 1

13. I love to tell amusing stories that illustrate my point at work, at home, or with friends.

    7 6 5 4 3 2 1

14. I sometimes act silly at unexpected times.

 7 6 5 4 3 2 1

15. I'm not uncomfortable laughing out loud with friends, family members, or co-workers.

 7 6 5 4 3 2 1

16. I use humor to help myself and others recall important things.

 7 6 5 4 3 2 1

If your score is from 100 to 112, you're either lying or can't add; a score between 90 and 99 indicates that you're a "humor pro"; 70–89 means minor adjustments may be in order for you; and 45–69 suggests that a major adjustment is needed.

If you didn't laugh or smile at my scoring method, give yourself a zero.

It's very important to make sure that your sense of humor isn't vanishing. One of the signs of recovery from clinical depression is the ability to see a bit of mirth from within. I suggest that you do a periodic humor check. It's not always easy to recognize it in yourself, so allow friends to give you an overview of your behavior.

Are you feeling too serious or down in the dumps? Getting help early on will offset what could become a serious condition. I've suffered from anxiety and depression, and I recommend avoiding it at all costs. Find a way to start laughing so you can start to rehabilitate yourself. If they take you away after you've had a nervous breakdown, they'll medicate you, put you in therapy, and make you color and weave baskets.

The reality of life on this earth is that you'll suffer. I know that sounds harsh, but it's part of every person's existence. My mantra has become: *Don't practice misery when it's not happening.* Create ways to entertain yourself as you move through the days of your life. Those tasks that feel the most mundane can be infused with humor and playfulness.

Driving in traffic is a wonderful way to chill out, listen to your favorite comic on a CD or the radio, or play music while singing your heart out. Standing in line at the supermarket—or any line, for that matter—is a perfect opportunity to connect and laugh with strangers. Make sure you watch funny movies often and especially do so with loved ones—it keeps life in balance. And don't take yourself too seriously no matter how old you are, because no one's getting out of here alive . . . you might just accelerate the process if you don't laugh often enough.

Ways to Wither

- Make every day a joyless experience. Follow the same routine and never deviate from your goals. If someone asks you to take a few minutes from your busy schedule to laugh or just hang out, don't do it!

- Give everyone around you lots of reasons to *not* feel good about being on the planet. Pepper your talks with facts about global warming, food contamination, pollution, war, and pestilence. If they try to counter with anything that sounds positive or upbeat, interrupt and barrage them with gloomy statistics.

- Allow yourself to get so uptight that you begin to look like a dead parrot.

Juicy Tidbits

- Watch as many funny, insightful movies as possible. Here are some of my personal favorites: *Being There* (1979), *The Full Monty* (1997), *Tootsie* (1982), *The Producers* (2005), and *Little Miss Sunshine* (2006).

- Join a group such as the Red Hat Society, where like-minded souls get together just to have fun.

- Take some improvisation classes to learn how to see humor in everyday life. It's also great for expanding your mind and thinking outside of the sandbox.

- Designate someone to be your humor buddy, and give them permission to let you know if you're losing your playfulness and ability to kid around.

- Let yourself go once in a while. If you have kids or grandchildren, allow them to lead you down the slippery slope to where you can act silly or "out of control." I don't have a problem in this area! I'm a firm believer in the old saying: "It's never too late to have a happy childhood."

STILL KICKIN'

WHY WE LOVE ROBERT DE NIRO

Well, how about we love him because he's one of the most mesmerizing actors of our time? Think about the fascinating characters he played in *The Godfather Part II, Taxi Driver, Raging Bull,* and *GoodFellas*—to name a few. It's scary just to watch him in action. When he's intimidating or roughing up another character on-screen, it's as if he's doing it to you!

But on the other hand, Robert is the guy who has a wonderful sense of humor about himself and has reached beyond his serious roles and cracked us up in the *Analyze This* and *Meet the Parents* movies . . . playing the tough guy gone wrong.

Most of all, maybe we love him because after September 11, 2001, this native New Yorker decided to do something to help Lower Manhattan recover from the devastating effects of the loss of the Twin Towers. So along with producer Jane Rosenthal, he introduced The Tribeca Film Festival. By the summer of 2002, the first festival took place and brought in over $10 million of income to local merchants; and during its second year, it raised an incredible $50 million.

The Tribeca Film Festival helped bring well-heeled crowds back to downtown Manhattan, and Robert achieved it through a program that supported both the arts and the community. How wonderful is that!

Chapter 11

How to Repair Your Soles

"We achieve inner health only through forgiveness—
the forgiveness not only of others but
also of ourselves."
— Joshua Loth Liebman

My childhood was spent in an idyllic setting up until the age of seven. If you've ever seen the movie *Moonstruck,* you'll have an idea of what my early life was like. We lived in a brownstone in Brooklyn filled with family, food, and eccentric characters who meandered through our house day and night. My mother and father worked, so I was left with my grandparents, Francesca and Lorenzo, who spent hours playing with me. They'd bake bread every day, and I was always part of the ritual in the kitchen. I had my own piece of dough that I'd create fun shapes with, and then I'd brush it with olive oil and sprinkle sesame seeds on top.

When it came out of the oven ready to eat, what joy and pride I felt!

My mother's best friends, Pepe and Lucy, lived across the street with their father. They had grown up on a houseboat because their father had been a sailor for the British navy. He spoke Sicilian with a limey accent and had a parrot who imitated him. Pepe was incredibly funny and would often help my mother clean the house. Her way to wash the kitchen floor was to strap brushes on the bottom of her feet and skate from one end to another. I loved being with her because she could imitate anyone.

I believe that Pepe had a profound influence on my own sense of humor. In addition to helping my mom clean, she'd take me to my ballet lessons every week—and then to Schrafft's for ice cream. Soon she began taking lessons herself, but eventually fell in love with flamenco dancing and became a world-class partner to José Greco. Years later when I was married, she came to visit, dressed to kill in all her Spanish finery. She also carried a shoulder bag that she never put down. The reason? It contained her bodyguard: a Chihuahua named Pepito. This dog was indeed Mighty Mouse himself. If he felt his mistress was in any danger, he emerged like a fiery dragon prepared to attack.

These memories have enabled me to build a foundation of sanity; however, the years to come were not nearly as heartwarming.

My days of innocence ended when my parents divorced. Within a short period, my mother remarried, sold the house in Brooklyn, and moved us into a home in the suburbs with her new husband. She never prepared me for the divorce *or* the remarriage, so I entered this new world without a single explanation. My entire support system vanished, except for my grandparents, who came with us but soon left due to the toxic atmosphere. Sadly, my mother had simply exchanged one emotionally distant man for another, with one exception: My father was essentially a depressed person who lived in his own inner hell, and my stepfather was often hell itself. As a result, I spent a great deal of my home life praying that his rage wouldn't surface.

I remember many a dinner feeling like it was a scene straight out of *Who's Afraid of Virginia Woolf?* As the sarcasm and castrating remarks escalated, my stepfather would overturn his chair and storm out of the room. After eating the rest of the meal in silence, I'd go to my room and enter the world of imagination. Much of my ability to entertain myself comes from my experiences during these times. I'd draw, write stories, and make up characters to play with. I also began to use humor as a way of softening the blows of a dysfunctional family life. I'd have my friends in hysterics as I mimicked the vicious fights between my mother and her husband. Viktor Frankl summed up my experience best: "Humor was another of the soul's weapons in the fight for self-preservation." Humor and parody had become an integral part of my ability to manage and cope with difficulties.

I often heard my mother complain about her second marriage and how unhappy she was. She'd jump from that to how enslaved she felt taking care of my grandparents. And when she wasn't festering about those issues, she'd moan about her job. As I got older, I'd offer suggestions: "Leave your husband—he's making you miserable!" "Send Grandma to your brother's for a month." "Get another job!" The response was always the same: "People will talk; I've already been divorced once." "I can't leave Grandma—they'll think I don't want her around." "How can I leave my job when we need the money?"

There was an element of truth in all her excuses, just as there is in so many of the choices we make concerning the situations in our own lives. But my mom chose to ignore the fact that she had options and choices. The misery she experienced every day and the tension in the house that was part of my daily life didn't make for a happy childhood.

My mom was also a crackerjack paralegal who could have been hired by many law firms but didn't feel secure enough to leave her current job. Her marriage created chaos, but divorce wasn't an option since she felt that "people would talk."

She had convinced herself that she was doing what was best for everyone, which made her feel righteous about her decisions, but essentially those choices only reinforced her innermost fears and prevented her from reaching her highest potential.

ꙮ ꙮ ꙮ

In the end, we all suffered. Our home was filled with anxiety, but life fell into a rhythm—albeit a rocky one. Then came more insanity. When I was 11, I was sexually abused by one of my uncles.

We were at a big family dinner—I think it was Thanksgiving. I remember my uncle asking me to leave the party and go to his house to feed his dog. And of course I went with him happily. I had no reason to be suspicious, and I loved dogs!

When we got there, he told me that my mother had talked to him and thought that I might have become sexually active. He then said that she had asked him to inspect me to see if I were still a virgin. This was just one incident, but he continued to pursue me for years.

This incredibly insidious setup would haunt me until I finally confronted my mother when I was in my 20s. Until then, I had not only been sexually abused, but lived with the impression that my mom had betrayed me in the most horrific way. She broke down and held me, repeating over and over that she would have never done that to me. I believed her, and it has allowed some of the pain to wash away. Since that moment, though, we never discussed it again.

It took years and years for me to resurrect a vivid memory of that event, but it's a well-known fact that individuals who are abused tend to dissociate from the experience in order to deal with its horror. Today, I can tell you the color of the carpet and what the dog looked like (a cocker spaniel). To have this person, a trusted uncle—who would take me places and play games with me—betray me like that was just unbelievable. It's still so ugly.

I remember that I had to just take the incident and stuff it into a drawer someplace. We went back to the dinner and both just sat down and the meal continued. Everybody else was eating and laughing, and it was so surreal. Life just went on. How can a child cope with something like that? I think for me—and many other victims who feel there's no one they can go to for help—it seemed like the only thing I could do was to pretend it never happened. After all, my uncle had told me that it was my mother who asked him to do it!

As a child, how was I supposed to explain such evil to myself? I couldn't digest it and just blocked it out, but there's a part of all of us that can't completely contain this kind of deception. Soon I began to have panic attacks. My pounding heart would wake me up, and I'd sit up clutching my blanket, not knowing what was happening. I'd call out to my mother and she'd try to calm me down, but neither one of us understood what was going on. She just thought I was anxious, and since she was a nervous person, she could relate. I never thought to tell her the truth because I believed she was a co-conspirator.

There's no humor inherent in a situation like this, but there's hope that one can find some kind of resolution through the mind's ability to reshape the horror into a model for resiliency. My mother didn't consciously try to harm me; she always did what she thought was best. Over the years and as a result of my work in mind/body medicine, I've grown to understand her and feel compassion toward her. But her behavior left me compromised in my ability to feel good about myself in certain areas of my life, and she never knew the extent of my pain and sorrow.

For example, I always felt diminished as a female in relationship to a male. I also thought that it was necessary to be perfect at everything in order to be loved; and to please people, I had to go to extremes so they'd care about me. In some ways, this attitude set me up to repeat the very behavior I took my mother to task for—I had become the victim of my own victimization! I've often found myself in situations where I've gone to great lengths to make someone happy only to find that *I* was miserable as a result.

When I got married the first time, I was barely 20, but I believed that it was going to give me what I never had as a child—a man who would love and adore me, and be a parent figure as well. I had no skills in the wife department. Who were my role models . . . the folks on *Leave It to Beaver?* Everything I saw firsthand about relationships stemmed from living in a psycho ward every day, hoping that someone would pass out drugs to the inmates to calm them down.

I had three children with my first husband, and even though I kept a clean house and fed them well, I couldn't possibly give them the emotional support they needed. I simply didn't have access to it within myself.

My second marriage was based on the fantasy that this person would be "the one," the savior who would once again give me the unconditional love I hadn't received from my father or stepfather. I wanted a husband who thought I was his princess. And I longed for—and sometimes still yearn for—the strong father figure who would take me in his arms and tell me that I was his special girl.

A great book for helping with forgiveness is *Forgive for Good: A Proven Prescription for Health and Happiness,* by Dr. Fred Luskin. Dr. Luskin offers a nine-step forgiveness method based on his groundbreaking studies into the healing powers and medical benefits of forgiveness. He's currently the cofounder and director of the Stanford University Forgiveness Project.

Our unfulfilled desires can lead us down some strange paths. My second husband and I couldn't sustain the relationship once I abandoned my role as June Cleaver and became *Loretta LaRoche.* June gave herself over, did everything for the sake of her man, and never once thought of herself. The males of my generation weren't acculturated to having wives who were successful in their own right. We also didn't have access to the myriad self-help products and counseling opportunities that are available to couples today. As I saw myself repeating the pattern and effectively becoming my mother—doing everything for my husband's sake and ignoring the things I needed—I not only became angry at my spouse but at myself, too.

Even when therapy was an option, his prototype for masculinity felt that it was "nobody else's business," and we should be able to figure things out ourselves. Many males who were born in the '30s and '40s were taught that "real" men don't reveal their innermost thoughts and feelings. I wish we had been able to go into therapy in the early years of our relationship—it would have saved us both a lot of agony. Many of our last years together were spent in a tug of war so filled with emotional angst that neither one of us was able to get what we needed to move forward. When we finally agreed to go into couples counseling, it was too late.

It finally became a no-brainer to get divorced. My body was in total rebellion: My joints constantly ached, and the sorrow I carried was unbearable. Nothing is worse than living with someone and feeling alone every day, and what made it seem even worse was that I knew I was at an age where divorce wasn't a place you wanted to visit.

When you're in your 60s and have been married for 23 years, you've acquired a lot of history. You've invested a great deal of time into the relationship, and you count on your mate to be there for you in your last act. Divorce deeply impacts your financial picture, as one or both of you will take a hit. But none of it matters if you're going to become ill or die from a situation that doesn't feed your spirit.

I thought I could escape my upbringing by promising myself that I'd make choices that were different from the ones my mother made, but how could that have happened when I wasn't even aware of how my childhood had affected my deepest levels of self?

You can't be aware of anything until you're awake. The worst part of not being in harmony with your inner self or trying to complete yourself through another person is that your mind, body, and soul start to wither. You need the juiciness that comes from being authentic. You can't feel your cells spurting with joy when you're contradicting your genuine self and basically living as a hypocrite.

I wasn't conscious of my own behavior until I went into therapy at age 60 and began the slow, painful process of realizing how deep my sorrows went. No one would ever recognize the pain I've carried because of my ability to counter those feelings with humor—I was my own *Pagliacci.* My therapist was always trying to point out how I had split myself into two women: one was the onstage personality who was confident and sassy, and the other was often crying out to be loved and would do anything to get affection. I learned that this type of behavior isn't unusual for victims of sexual abuse and for those who've suffered through dysfunctional family lives.

The baggage of the past can negate your abilities to age well in body, mind, and spirit. You're a product of your history, but you don't have to live as if you've been petrified in time. You have the power to learn from the past, live with joy in the present, and have high hopes for the future!

Let's look at some ways to help you heal; grow; and start living a juicy, vibrant life.

Poetry Therapy

"Poetry is not a turning loose of emotion, but an escape from emotion; it is not the expression of personality, but an escape from personality.

But, of course, only those who have personality
and emotions know what it means to want
to escape from these things."
— T. S. Eliot

"For those who are suffering and seek counseling,
the task of writing poetry is more than an escape;
it is a transformation from their emotions.
And for those who read poetry as clients, it is
a way of articulating the challenges
they need to face and overcome."
— Charles R. Figley, Ph.D.,
Florida State University Traumatology Institute

Reading and writing poetry can be a very effective tool for healing and personal growth. Here's a list of poems recommended by the National Association for Poetry Therapy that are commonly used in therapy:

1. "The Journey," by Mary Oliver
2. "Autobiography in Five Short Chapters," by Portia Nelson
3. "The Armful," by Robert Frost
4. "The Rubáiyát of Omar Khayyám"
5. "If I Should Cast Off This Tattered Coat," by Stephen Crane

6. "The Road Not Taken," by Robert Frost
7. "Self-Improvement Program," by Judith Viorst
8. "Variation on a Theme by Rilke," by Denise Levertov
9. "The Man in the Glass," by Elton Evans
10. "I Knew This Kid," by James Kavanaugh
11. "Marks," by Linda Pastan
12. "Talking to Grief," by Denise Levertov
13. "The Truth in 1963," by Edgar Allen Imhoff
14. "Message," by Carol Bernstern
15. "This is Just to Say," by William Carlos Williams
16. "Impasse," by Langston Hughes
17. "I Can't Go On," by Dory Previn
18. "One Art," by Elizabeth Bishop
19. "Swineherd," by Eilean Ni Chuilleanain
20. "I Wandered Lonely as a Cloud," by William Wordsworth
21. "A Ballad of Dreamland," by Algernon Charles Swinburne
22. "The Summer Day," by Mary Oliver

You may not feel drawn to reading poetry or writing some yourself. Still, it's worth a try, and it's not as difficult as you may think. Pick one of the "poetic stems" below, put your pen to paper, and simply go with the flow. Don't stop even if you don't like what you're writing; you can go always go back and fix it later. Just get something written down . . . those first words just might be a path toward healing:

I'm most happy when . . .
Love is . . .
What matters most . . .
I feel loved when . . .
My greatest strength is . . .
My heart yearns for . . .
I find joy in . . .
My yesterdays have shown me . . .
I feel close to you until . . .
I feel lonely when . . .

I thought I'd give it a shot myself, so here's my first foray into being a poetess. These words resonate deep from within and reflect on my dysfunctional childhood.

My adult is learning to embrace the happiness I felt as a child before the sorrow came to visit.
He entered without permission and stayed too long.

I finally gave him notice, but his ghost
often appears.
I plead with him to leave, but it is I who
must banish the tears of the past and
replace them with the joy of knowing
that if he comes again, I can choose to
not open the door.
Because now I know the difference.

Still Kickin'

Why We Love Maya Angelou

Maya Angelou mesmerized the nation in 1993 with the reading of her stirring, exciting, compelling, wistful, and, ultimately, hopeful poem "On the Pulse of Morning," written for the inauguration of President Bill Clinton.

It was a triumphant moment for the woman whose autobiographical book *I Know Why the Caged Bird Sings,* published in the late 1960s, shocked the country with its honest and poignant portrait of a young black girl facing injustice and brutality. It's a beautiful, lyrical story that shows the strength of the human spirit, but its message is more powerful than some people in this country wanted to hear—so they tried to silence it. Even today, it's regularly on the list of books banned from public and school libraries.

Maya is a woman who doesn't have a formal college education but speaks several languages. And not only is she an award-winning poet and novelist, but she's a screenwriter, director, teacher, historian, and civil-rights activist. She's also an accomplished actress, performing wide-ranging roles in films from the epic miniseries *Roots* to the 2006 comedy *Madea's Family Reunion* (at the age of 78).

Her amazing talents and wisdom and unfailing ability to find beauty even in the brutal have given hope and inspiration to millions.

Resiliency

Through 15 years of groundbreaking research, Karen Reivich and Andrew Shatté, two expert psychologists and the country's preeminent resilience research team, have concluded that resilience is what determines how high people rise above what threatens to wear them down. I've always thought of this quality as a person's ability to bounce back from life's hardships by transforming them into challenges. Being resilient allows individuals to survive in this chaotic world with elegance and grace.

Many of us tend to become the victims of old thought patterns that don't serve us well. We have more than 60,000 thoughts a day; and if we're not vigilant about controlling how we think, we can become enveloped in a "thought tsunami." It's much easier to just maintain the way we've always thought than to try to consciously change deeply ingrained behaviors.

We can't control what happens to us, but we can control our reactions and how we think about situations. This capacity isn't handed to us through our genetics; it's actually a learned psychological skill. Individuals who practice resiliency have developed the ability to push through problems rather than allowing difficulties to overwhelm and push *them* around. Resilient people have realized that their mind can become an ally—instead of the enemy—during tough times.

The following are some techniques to help you walk the resiliency trail:

1. Remember that a thought can be latched onto or let go. It can't disturb you unless you let it.
2. Think of times when you showed courage in the face of adversity. You've been the hero or heroine of your own saga many times. Who is that person who triumphs over difficulty? Create a

pseudonym for this strong being. Resonate with your inner warrior. Perhaps when things get rough, you call upon Theresa the Tenacious or Betsy Braveheart or Wanda the Wonderful and ask for guidance.

3. Create an attitude of strength, and learn to walk purposefully. You send yourself and those around you "wimp messages" when your body language looks as if you just spent two years in a dungeon with only bread and water for sustenance. Stand tall and your mind will follow!

4. Keep in mind that millions of people throughout history have endured extraordinarily difficult or horrific circumstances and survived to tell their tale. Keep some books next to your bed that illustrate the stories of some of these courageous individuals. I often highlight passages and reread them when I'm feeling vulnerable.

   Here are some of my favorites:

   Man's Search For Meaning, by Viktor E. Frankl

   Left to Tell: Discovering God Amidst the Rwandan Holocaust, by Immaculée Ilibagiza

   Night, by Elie Weisel

The Measure of a Man, by Sidney Poitier

Lessons in Becoming Myself,
by Ellen Burstyn

Escape from Slavery, by Francis Bok

God Grew Tired of Us, by John Bul Dau

5. Build a circle of individuals who help you in your quest for solutions rather than those who enable you to stay stuck in the limbo of impossibilities.

Narrative Repair

Finding meaning in suffering can help an individual see a difficult experience as a challenge and allows him or her to focus on the positive aspects of the situation. Many cancer patients and survivors have discovered that life becomes sweeter, their troublesome relationships are healed, and they become more empathetic toward others who are going through hard times. Surprisingly, many people who suffer from serious diseases or illnesses find that their gratitude barometer reaches an all-time high.

Narrative Repair is a process in which you tell your own story, diminishing the power of the trauma and highlighting the qualities of your life that demonstrate strength and resiliency. By reframing your story in such a way, healing can begin.

My dear friend Ann Webster, of the Benson-Henry Institute for Mind Body Medicine at Massachusetts General Hospital, tells a wonderful story about a female cancer patient who was devastated by the thought of losing her hair during chemotherapy.

In order to overcome her grief, she bought herself a very lovely wig that she wore almost all the time. Once while attending a banquet, another woman came up to her and said, "I just love that chic haircut of yours! Where did you get it done?" And the woman replied, "Darling, you'll never know. This is the most expensive hairdo you could possibly imagine."

Now, when discussing her feelings about hair loss, the woman shares that positive story. It's something that makes her feel *good* about the experience . . . and that alone helps healing.

Journal Writing

One of the most powerful ways to help people repair their stories is through writing. James W. Pennebaker, a psychologist at the University of Texas, has been studying the health benefits of writing about personal trauma and has found that the act of putting one's emotional upheavals into words and onto paper results in improved physical and emotional well-being. He also states that by converting painful emotions and images into words, we make them more manageable because we change the way we organize and think about them. By integrating the thoughts and feelings, we're more easily able to construct a coherent narrative of the experience. Then the event can be summarized, stored, or forgotten.

Music to Soothe the Soul

My mind just loves to dwell on stuff, especially when I feel that there's been an injustice, but I've found that music enables me to soothe my swirling thoughts. Research shows that music provides relief to individuals who experience negative cognition, intrusive thoughts, or dysphoria (a state of unease or mental discomfort). After hearing music, people are less threatened by stimuli that might trigger phobic reactions. I find that my mind clears when I listen to "Simply Irresistible," by Robert Palmer. I also love Broadway songs, and my new favorite is "Always Look on the Bright Side of Life" from the musical *Spamalot*. Whenever I feel my mind trying to dive into the snake pit of "awfulizing" situations, I turn on my iPod and sing along to those upbeat tunes as they lift my spirits.

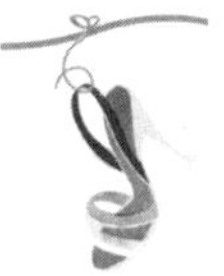

Prayers for Letting Go

I've also found some incredible inspiration and healing in my Buddhist readings. They've shown me that those who have harmed me suffer, too. To include those individuals in your prayers takes courage, but it brings you down the path of forgiveness and increases your ability to let go of old hurts. Angry or fearful energy that you put forth perpetuates past or present injuries and can endanger your health.

Here's an empowering Buddhist prayer and exercise to help heal, let go, and spread loving-kindness.

Make yourself comfortable and quiet your thoughts. Focus on this ancient prayer:

> *May I be free from fear.*
> *May I be free from suffering.*
> *May I be happy.*
> *May I be filled with loving-kindness.*

Now shift your concentration from yourself to someone you care about, and say this prayer for his or her well-being.

Then think of acquaintances or individuals whom you don't know at all and recite these wishes for them.

Last, and most important, recall a person you dislike or don't get along with. Open your heart and repeat the prayer. Say the words aloud, and feel your capacity for empathy and forgiveness. Know that your spirit overflows with compassion and love.

And you can find comfort in the "Prayer of Saint Francis," attributed to St. Francis of Assisi:

Lord, make me an instrument of Your peace.
Where there is hatred, let me sow love;
Where there is injury, pardon;
Where there is doubt, faith;
Where there is despair, hope;
Where there is darkness, light;
Where there is sadness, joy.
O Divine Master, grant that I may not so much seek to be consoled as to console;
To be understood as to understand;
To be loved as to love;
For it is in giving that we receive;
It is in pardoning that we are pardoned;
And it is in dying that we are born to eternal life.
Amen.

Chapter 12

You Gotta Love Your Heels

"Age does not protect you from love.
But love, to some extent, protects you from age."
— Jeanne Moreau

We live in a society that uses the word *love* to describe anything and everything. We love candy, TV, and beer; we love our pets, our yards, our children, our mates, and who knows what else. We're inundated with movies, books, and music that speak of eternal love, love lost, and unrequited love. Because of this obsession, most of the women of my generation were brought up waiting for their Prince Charming—the rescuer and star of our popular myths. And once he professed his true love, the lucky girl was guaranteed to live a happy, fulfilled life.

I certainly believed it! I thought I was going to be swept off my feet and whisked to the land of eternal romance . . . but the only "sweeping" I got was when I swept the front porch.

In recent years, we've exchanged the prince for the pursuit of the "soul mate," the one who will be our perfect match and make us feel that now at last we're complete. Once again, though, this is leaving us in the victim position; unless we can find our other half, we can't be whole.

At this stage in my life, I realize that partners should be just that—mates who join us and combine their strengths, talents, and values with ours so we can lead a wonderful life together. However, if these individuals don't show up, we can still be complete without them. We don't need them to survive and thrive—they're merely the icing on the cake.

I've felt the passion of love and experienced firsthand the resulting chaos it leaves in its wake, but if the infatuation segues into something more lasting and fulfilling, then you're indeed fortunate. Because falling in love is a form of insanity, it often becomes the curtain behind which more important issues hide, such as whether you have any values in common—or if perhaps your lover is actually a vampire who will suck you dry.

How many times have you seen talk shows that spotlight couples who remain in relationships together despite abuse or addictive behavior? When these individuals are asked why they stay, you often hear, "Well, I love him (or her)," or something to that effect. This isn't love; it's merely another manifestation of addiction.

Amazingly, the brain circuitry that's activated when a person is infatuated with another matches that of a drug addict who's desperately seeking a fix. Lovers become totally illogical and fail to see any of their mates' shortcomings because their minds are bathed in oxytocin, dopamine, estrogen, and testosterone. The early sensations of love are analogous to the high that one feels while on opiates such as cocaine, heroin, or morphine. It's no wonder that people believe they're capable of doing anything or going anywhere in order to be with their beloved. I've been there, and it wreaked havoc on my life.

There's nothing like the intensity of being completely enamored with someone, but if you have a legacy of abandonment and abuse, you're in big trouble. You can't freely give your partner what you haven't been given. In other words, if you've come from a home where tenderness was meagerly doled out or not provided at all, you've suffered the cruelest type of deprivation. And if that's what you learned, how can you know how to express or receive love in a healthy manner? If you've been sexually or emotionally abused, you'll more than likely do everything in your power to be in a loving relationship, even though your understanding of what love really is has been tampered with and is now skewed. Your behavior toward yourself and others will reek of insecurity, and you'll suffer from physical and mental problems as you stumble from one unhealthy relationship to the next.

You need affection in order to flourish and thrive and stay fully alive. Nothing feeds the mind, body, and soul like loving and being loved; however, there are different types of love, and the most important thing to understand is which kind replenishes you and which depletes you. I've experienced both.

Deep, meaningful love is being able to give to another without losing your essential self. For many people, it's a line that's very difficult to see.

It's imperative to express affection and feel cherished as you get older. You can focus your love on a partner, family members, pets, friends, or perhaps individuals you support through your volunteer work. People who age brilliantly have discovered how important this facet of their life is, but if you've felt that you didn't get the love you needed in the past or don't have it now, there's still hope.

Since my divorce, I've discovered that my cat, Llama, also known as Mr. Boo, is an incredible source of love and companionship. I'd also adore having a partner to share the rest of my life with, but I'll no longer compromise my values to simply have the "fix" of romance. If that were to happen, it would be wonderful, but I've realized as I plow through this journey that I don't have to have a mate in order to feel fulfilled and connected to others. Mr. Boo is more than a good pet; he's a teacher, a friend, and a constant source of unconditional love. I believe he came into my life to show me that love doesn't have to be as complex as I've made it out to be.

Being a victim of sexual abuse taught me to believe that I had to give everything of myself to be loved. But Mr. Boo simply wants me to fill his food bowl, pet him, and play with him from time to time. In exchange, he purrs every time I approach him, greets me at the door when I come home, and dutifully sleeps at the foot of my bed. And when he senses that I'm sad or distraught, he lies next to me and stares at me as if he knows what I'm feeling.

In the last several years, researchers have found that taking care of pets can help reduce blood pressure, and they're also an excellent source of comfort to elderly people. I used to think that people who were over the top about their pets were a little crazy. For example, my friend Myra is a cat lover; and once when her cat was missing, she hung posters everywhere and was beside herself until she found him. At the time I didn't understand how she could be so devastated—I never thought of owning pets because my ex-husband was allergic to them—but now I totally get it.

I feel blessed to have grown closer to my children. Despite divorces and other problems that upset our lives, we've managed to emerge from the storm and are able to share many loving moments together.

Grandchildren can be a great source of love, too. I've never thought of myself as a grandmother, and in many ways I'm not the stereotypical grandma. I was just 46 when my granddaughter Amanda was born; and shortly after that, my daughter gave birth to her son Tyler. I remember thinking, *This can't be true. I'm too young!* My own grandmother had gray hair and a physique like a dumpling. She always wore an apron, and her arms had little wings underneath that waved in the breeze as she moved about. Her couture was a flowered dress, oxford shoes, and the eternal presence of her cherished rosary beads that she wrapped around her wrist. Her days were filled with cooking, cleaning, and making sure everyone was okay. I didn't come close to this vision . . . and my career was just taking off!

On top of that, two of my children lived in another state, so it wasn't easy to just stop by for a visit or offer to babysit for them. I know my children haven't always been happy with my skills as a grandmother, and perhaps I could have been better at it. But in my defense, I feel that the times haven't caught up to the fact that society has redefined how grandparents function today.

Chaka Khan is a grandmother; and Suzanne Somers, Roseanne Barr, and Goldie Hawn have grandkids, too. We're hipper, and more invested in living as juicy a life as possible. I also know that if I hadn't experienced the blessing of my work—which has gifted me with the awareness of healing the past in order to live more fully in the present—I wouldn't have the wonderful relationships I enjoy with my grandchildren today. I wasn't the "get on the floor and roll around with the kids" kind of grandma, but I'm great with the older ones. They think I'm cool, and we have fantastic times together. I have 11 grandkids now! I'm able to share myself with them in ways I couldn't as a mother; and due to healing therapy and my life's work, I've been able to love and be loved in a much better fashion.

Contemplate these questions: *Who are the individuals I really care about? Why do I love them? How do I feel when I'm around them?* Do you feel nurtured, or perhaps neglected? Think of the people you've loved—positive and negative relationships—and what you've learned from the kind of affection they gave you. Do you see any patterns that you don't want to repeat? Do you seek love and approval only from others and not from within? Have you realized that you can be loved just by being yourself?

Juicy Tidbits

- In a recent *National Geographic* article about the science of love, Lauren Slater interviewed anthropologist and Rutgers University professor Helen Fisher and her colleagues Arthur Aron and Lucy Brown about their fascinating research. They were interested in seeing how the brain reacts when a person is in love, and their findings could help explain why people behave in certain ways when they're deeply infatuated:

> Fisher and her colleagues . . . recruited subjects who had been "madly in love" for an average of seven months. Once inside the MRI machine, subjects were shown two photographs, one neutral, the other of their loved one.
>
> What Fisher saw fascinated her. When each subject looked at his or her loved one, the parts of the brain linked to reward and pleasure . . . lit up.

- Donatella Marazziti, a professor of psychiatry at the University of Pisa in Italy, has studied the biochemistry of lovesickness, and the similarities between love and obsessive-compulsive disorder (OCD). After taking blood samples from individuals who were newly in love and people who were diagnosed with OCD, she discovered that the levels of serotonin in both groups were 40 percent lower than in subjects who didn't suffer from OCD and weren't in the early stages of a romantic relationship. Infatuation and OCD may have a similar profile!

- In long-term relationships, oxytocin—a hormone that promotes feelings of connection and bonding—is believed to be abundant in both partners. You can help emit this substance by hugging or having sex. But that's not the only way to release this hormone—treat yourself to a spa visit and embrace the calming, revitalizing feelings you can experience by getting a professional massage.

Still Kickin'

Why We Love Nora Ephron

Okay, how could you not love a woman in her 60s who writes a book called *I Feel Bad about My Neck?*

From behind the scenes, Nora Ephron has been making us laugh for decades. She was the screenwriter of wildly successful comedies such as *Sleepless in Seattle* and *When*

Harry Met Sally . . . (yes, it was Nora who imagined the famous "I'll have what she's having" restaurant scene).

She's been in the forefront as well, as a celebrated essayist and novelist who's mined some of the most intimate and painful details of her life and transformed them into refreshing, comedic material.

Read Nora's book or see the film version of her incredible work *Heartburn*—a fictional account of her marriage to Carl Bernstein, who dumped her for another woman while Nora was pregnant.

For her fabulous talent, for her courage and ability to stay juicy and lighthearted no matter what life hands her, and for writing perhaps the most wonderful revenge story ever told, we kick up our heels to Nora!

ൈ ൈ ൈ ൈ ൈ ൈ

Chapter 13

How Many Times Do I Resole Before I Buy a New Pair?

"I want to die young at a ripe old age."
— Ashley Montagu

I'm amused by how many times I hear people comparing natural versus unnatural aging. The latest and greatest way to sell beauty products and services is to call them *anti-aging*. Anti-aging doesn't sound like such a good idea to me . . . either you age or you die. It's that simple! Nothing is going to stop the inevitable, but there are so many options that can help improve the process of growing older and make it more enjoyable. And now there's even research confirming that men and women who *perceive* themselves as young are physically and mentally healthier than those who don't.

What I find disconcerting about all this is that many people, especially females, have decided to take sides on what they believe to be the right and wrong ways of aging. Some individuals view plastic surgery as a pact with the devil; and if you go under the knife, you cross the line and make a bargain for eternal life with the evil one. These folks feel they must embrace their wrinkles, gray hair, and other withering parts—no questions asked.

The opposing camp isn't only *willing* to have surgery, but they'll try anything that fills in, plumps up, or lifts their bodies. They're on a quest to defy the onslaught of aging.

If you go too far in either direction, you'll start looking like a parody of yourself. *Natural* doesn't have to mean that you'll end up resembling an old shrew from one of Grimms' fairy tales, and *unnatural* doesn't imply that you'll be transformed into a mannequin at Bloomingdale's.

There's a middle ground, and there's also the option of just acknowledging that you can do whatever floats your boat without guilt. But feeling okay about your decision is difficult when you're bombarded by books touting anti-aging miracles and gorgeous celebrities chattering on TV about the latest quick fix. Then you change the channel and hear the opposite opinion, stressing the value of going gray and loving yourself as you are—as if any of those methods constitute the one true path to nirvana.

It's all so silly. Personally, I don't care who does what! If you want to put your face on backward or move your butt up to your neck, go for it. Or if you'd rather let your hair turn gray and grow past your kneecaps so you can be the next Rapunzel, then hooray for you, too. I happen to fall into the camp of wanting to look young as I age, but I didn't always feel that way.

Long before it became commonplace, a friend of mine had a face-lift. I thought she was so vain and selfish to spend money to "fix" her face. At that point, my arrogance forgot to inform me that someday *I* might also consider having some plastic surgery. I remember my professorial self chiding my girlfriend about the possibility that she could die on the table, leaving her family bereft just because she wanted to appear more attractive. She gave me a huge grin and said at least she'd look good in the coffin.

I had visions of her coming out of surgery with her eyes on top of her forehead and her cheeks swept back as if she'd just come out of a wind tunnel. But she looked great! Before the surgery, we seemed close to the same age; afterward, it was pretty clear that I appeared to be about ten years older than she was, and I hated it. No matter how hard I tried, I couldn't reconcile myself to the fact that my eyelids were starting to cover my eyes—even when I wasn't sleeping—and they always felt tired and heavy. And not only did I have bags under my eyes, but they were packed and ready to go on a three-week trip to China. I finally decided to at least get a consultation.

My biggest issue about the surgery was knowing that the doctor would have to put me under. I can't stand the thought of anesthesia because I'm a control freak who has to be in charge of everything. However, I discovered that even though I'd be sedated, I would still be semi-awake in a "twilight sleep." I did some research and found an incredibly gifted surgeon in Boston who's certified by the American Board of Plastic Surgery (which is a must, by the way), and he answered all my questions and helped me feel comfortable about the procedure. I had also heard many positive things about his work.

So I bit the bullet. Believe me, for days before I went in, I imagined every possible horrific thing that could go wrong during the surgery. My mind can go to very scary places! I pictured the scene at my funeral with my kids crying and saying, "But she looked just fine." And I also envisioned myself surviving the surgery and walking into a room as children ran out past me in horror after a look at my newly deformed face.

Fortunately, all went well and my eyes look really good. Since then I've tried microdermabrasion, Restylane, and most recently, Botox. Millions of men and women turn to Botox to erase wrinkles, but can removing frown lines actually cause individuals to *feel* happier—in addition to looking better?

I find it fascinating that Charles Darwin first suggested the idea that facial muscles and skin movement might contribute to our moods and sense of well-being. Based on this notion, Eric Finzi, M.D., Ph.D., and Erika Wasserman, Ph.D., set out to see if alleviating people's furrowed brows could impact depressive disorders.

During their study, ten clinically depressed patients between the ages of 36 and 63 who had never been treated with Botox were given injections directly into the frown muscles (between the eyebrows). Two months after the treatment, nine of the ten subjects were no longer considered depressed.

I'm sure some of you are thinking that being in a good mood doesn't matter if you're going to die from the procedure that's supposed to help you. I wasn't ever going to try Botox because I didn't want to look like some of the stars who've lost all expression and look like wax dummies. However, when it's applied correctly, it simply minimizes lines and makes you look more rested.

I've also read that individuals who've had plastic surgery view themselves as younger; therefore, they act younger and their bodies somehow benefit with improved immunity. But these types of outcomes aren't hard facts and must be studied for longer periods of time, and on more people. Until then, though, I like the idea of looking younger as

I'm getting older! I just hope I don't transform into *The Picture of Dorian Gray.*

Once again, I'm not suggesting that this is for everyone. Do whatever feels most authentic to your values but avoid attaining a cultlike mentality. Catch yourself before uttering, "I'd never . . ." because if you change your mind one day, those words will come back to haunt you. Whatever you decide, make sure you do your homework and choose qualified professionals. Check their credentials and request some testimonials from their clients. Many horrible procedures have been performed on individuals who were so desperate to look better that they rushed into things and ended up terribly botched up—or dead.

If a doctor's office advertises that they can cure warts, lift your butt, and invest your stock portfolio, then *something is wrong.* If you find yourself in a place where they're doing low-cost breast implants and it happens to be in the back of an auto mechanic shop, *run—don't walk.* Frankenstein already has a bride!

As you age, it also makes sense to reevaluate your hair, makeup, and clothing. You don't want to start looking like a checkout girl in an outpost in Siberia. There are many wonderful styles that can make you feel current, vital, and somewhat hip; and I've often told my grandchildren that if they ever see me looking really decrepit, they need to haul me off to a makeover retreat. Sometimes you don't realize when you're slipping into the black hole of wardrobe hell. You might have looked cute 20 years ago in your push-up bra and tight jeans, but are you sure you still do today? Your jeans may be choking the living hell out of your thighs, and your breasts may need more than just a push *up*—they might need a crane!

I've noticed some pretty frightening hairdos on women who should have given up the "look" after Bette Davis died. And the dye jobs that make your head look like a Brillo pad gone mad need to go, too. There are fantastic products on the market that allow you to achieve a beautiful hair color—you can create a look that's sublime or edgy, according to your mood. Or you can stick with your natural hue. I've seen a lot of exquisite gray-haired individuals, but you have to maintain it. If it starts to yellow, people might think you have jaundice.

Cover the basics, too: Moisturize your skin and practice good oral hygiene. Taking care of your teeth isn't just a vanity issue—not doing so can seriously jeopardize your health. More and more studies confirm the correlation between periodontal problems and heart disease. The mouth is the conduit for bacteria to travel into arteries, which will then create plaque and can eventually lead to heart attacks and strokes. In addition, yellow teeth aren't very appealing and can be made to look whiter. But avoid bleaching them so much that they can double as a laser beam.

Make sure you get a good night's sleep. If you're suffering from insomnia (and that can mean having difficulty when you first try to fall asleep or that you wake up after a few hours and are unable to get back to sleep) and it lasts for more than two weeks, see a physician who specializes in sleep disorders. Don't get hooked on sleeping pills! Meditation, cognitive behavioral therapy, and altering sleeping habits are techniques that have been proven to be far more effective than drugs. Getting your zzz's is a critical aspect to not only looking healthy, but for proper immune function and improved memory. So make your bedroom a cozy haven for rest, renewal, and other pleasant activities.

Finally, wear sunblock every day. I used to tan, but I stopped 15 years ago because I didn't want to look like a leather pocketbook—or a snake's cousin.

There are tons of terrific things you can do to look and feel as good as possible. You just have to have the desire, time, and money . . . it's up to you. At the very least, keep an open mind and investigate your options so you can make informed decisions. I can almost guarantee that if you look well, you'll be empowered to age well, too.

Still Kickin'

Why We Love Jane Fonda

How can anyone not admire a woman who has beautifully reinvented herself as many times as Jane Fonda has? She's assumed many different personas while always remaining elegant and classic. From sex-symbol actress (who remembers *Barbarella?*); to anti-war protester and right-wing whipping girl; to exercise guru (*Jane Fonda's Workout* remains one of the most successful exercise videos ever); to Academy Award–winning actress (remember her stunning performances in *Klute, Coming Home,* and *The China Syndrome,* among many others?); to passionate activist; and best-selling author.

But these days, Jane has morphed all aspects of herself into one fully formed, well-rounded woman whose complex history makes her a fascinating individual who demands respect and admiration. She has publicly apologized for her past errors in judgment (most notably, the infamous Hanoi Jane photo during the Vietnam War) and works tirelessly to promote liberal and feminist causes she believes in.

After a more than decadelong hiatus, she resumed her acting career at age 68. She's also written a stylish and honest autobiography. Once again, Jane has managed to overcome negative perceptions and reinvigorate and redefine her public image; and she does it in a way that so few celebrities can—by being true to who she is and what she cares about whether or not those views are popular. Jane remains a vital and powerful voice in American popular culture.

CHAPTER 14

WALK TALL INTO THE FUTURE

"Human life is a schoolroom. Take the curriculum."
— Emmanuel (as channeled by Pat Rodegast)

Our lives are like a university, and every day we have the opportunity to take a class in how to make the most of our experiences. Depending on how well we learn, we can develop skills that create a life filled with possibility . . . or one filled with pain. Yes, there are many situations that are simply beyond our control, but *we* can determine how to react to and handle them—and that's the most important lesson we can ever learn.

Much of aging is based on adaptation, which helps foster resiliency. How have we dealt with the bumps and lumps that come with the gift of life? What have we done with the treasures we picked up along the way? Although my family has gone through many tough times, I've been fortunate to have witnessed them endure every hardship with humor and incredible grit. My grandparents were immigrants who left their native country and familiar customs in order to start over in America. What drove my grandfather's desire to come here was his dream of opening an Italian bakery and pasteria. He fulfilled his wishes only to have them dashed when he lost his right arm due to gangrene. Unfortunately, penicillin hadn't yet been discovered.

Because of my grandfather's disability, when my mother was just 14, she learned to be an expert typist and began supporting her parents. She eventually became a paralegal and was a secretary to many high-powered lawyers on Wall Street, including Jacob Javits. Our family survived the Depression because of my mother's frugality. She later bought a brownstone in Brooklyn, and the whole family moved in—I'm talking aunts, uncles, cousins . . . anyone who couldn't afford a place to live. The characters' home life in the recent film *Little Miss Sunshine* was a dish of spumoni compared to us. Our dwelling became a boardinghouse of sorts and a wonderful potpourri of individuals for me to hang out with and learn from.

I watched my family live with gusto despite their disputes and physical ailments. No amount of asthma could deter my grandfather from making his rounds of the neighborhood to check in on his cronies. And my mother went to work just like a postal carrier—neither wind, nor rain, nor snow could prevent her from getting to the office on time. She had terrible lower-back pain, and I'd often see her heading to work in the morning standing upright but returning looking like a human question mark. My grandmother suffered daily with arthritis, yet she always made sure we had wonderful meals. The messages I got over and over from them was: "Don't give up!" To this day, I'd say that one of my greatest strengths is perseverance.

As I mentioned earlier, there were also many unhappy incidents and dysfunctional situations in my family life, but I learned from those experiences as well. The key to my breaking the negative cycle occurred when I examined those times and recognized that I had choices—I could *choose* not to repeat them.

Self-reflection is necessary throughout life, but even more so as we get older. Through my years of teaching and lecturing, I've listened to many people agonize about their pasts and the pain and suffering they experienced. I've realized that it's necessary to revisit some situations in order to process and learn from them; however, our society seems stuck on dwelling on our angst.

Oprah *and* Ellen are about the only talk-show hosts who focus on how individuals can be victorious, successful, and fulfilled despite one's shortcomings or backgrounds. The rest make some attempts but spend the majority of their airtime exhibiting wounded people and their tormentors. We also have few, if any, forums for interaction between our youth and older people who have much life experience to pass on. Wouldn't more open dialogue be incredibly informative and inspiring? Let's hope this will change as the boomers age, but it's going to take time.

We need the wisdom of the generations who lived before us. Native Americans and other cultures have deeply revered tribal elders who patiently instruct the young members of their community. Knowledge is the gift that keeps on giving as we age . . . if we put forth the effort and do the work.

I've created the following questionnaire for juicy aging as a way for you to examine how the past has influenced your present experiences—good, bad, or indifferent—and how you might take what you know now to brighten your future.

As you answer the questions on a separate piece of paper, or just in your own mind, I hope you'll find that the road map you design helps you find your way to a life filled with more juice and joy than you could imagine!

Questionnaire for Juicy Aging

1. Where did you live as a child, and who were your primary caregivers?
2. What type of experiences can you recall? Did you feel safe, loved, supported, and cared for; or was it a struggle? Perhaps it was somewhere in the middle. Describe those early memories in detail if possible.
3. Who were the most nurturing people in your life: your mother, father, grandparents, aunts, uncles, neighbors? Why? What specific things did they do to make you feel loved?
4. Who were the most demanding, controlling, hurtful, or abusive individuals you encountered?
5. What types of behavior did their actions elicit? Anger, hysteria, sadness, sarcasm?
6. What kinds of things did you do as a child? For example, did you paint, sew, dance, play an instrument, act, or participate in sports? Do you do any of these hobbies now?
7. Did you do any kinds of activities with your family? Can you remember any particular vacation or event that really stands out? Why do you think it's so prominent in your memory?

8. Who was your first love? What attracted you to him or her?
9. How many other romantic partners have there been? Do you remember their names and why you were drawn to them? What did you learn from these individuals?
10. When did you have your first sexual experience? How did you feel afterward? Do you feel comfortable with your sexuality? If not, why?
11. Are (or were) you married or in a long-term relationship? Have you been married more than once? Was the marriage (or marriages) everything you'd hoped for?
12. Do you have children? Can you see yourself in them?
13. Have you found yourself repeating your parents' behavior? Are they positive or negative habits? Did you improve on how they handled parenting, or did you become their clone?
14. Have you ever been in therapy? Was it helpful?
15. Have you worked on letting go and forgiving anything your parents might have done that wasn't in your best interest? If not, why haven't you?

16. What types of relationships do you have with your own children? Could improvements be made?
17. What have you learned from your significant others, kids, parents, friends, or co-workers?
18. If you have a partner, is your relationship satisfying? Are you growing together?
19. Do you take care of yourself? Have you always done so? How does your mental/spiritual/physical self feel today?
20. What kind of lifestyle changes could you make to improve your well-being?
21. What kind of work do you do, or are you retired? Does your work or leisure time bring you joy and happiness? Have you found your passion? If not, why haven't you?
22. Do you have a spiritual practice? Can you describe it?
23. Do you have elderly parents who need your care? How does this impact you? Would you want to be cared for in the same way? What emotions do you sense from within when you're around them? Do you feel vulnerable or fearful about your own possible frailties?

24. Do you have a support system of individuals who validate your feelings and will help guide you through the coming years? If so, who are these people, and what do they contribute to your life?
25. Are you feeling financially secure? If not, what are you doing to change your situation? Are all your documents in order, such as wills, trusts, and so on? Do you have a health-care proxy, and does this individual know your wishes?
26. What lessons have you gleaned from answering these questions? Have you shifted your perceptions about what you need, what type of individuals you seek out, or what the meaning of your life is at this particular point?
27. What kinds of strengths have you gained as a result of your life experiences?
28. How would you describe yourself at this time in your life?
29. Are you where you want to be?
30. What are your dreams, goals, and intentions? How and when do you plan to manifest them? And if not now, when will you begin?

It might be interesting to share this experience with friends. Have everyone answer the questions in advance, and then set up a group dialogue and see where it goes.

We often discuss the events in our lives in short bursts of conversation, but to really focus on where we want to go from here—and how to get there—takes understanding, effort, and courage. And don't forget to laugh along the way. Terminal living isn't an option!

ᘏ ᘏ ᘏ ᘏ ᘏ ᘏ

EPILOGUE

TRY TO STAY ON YOUR TOES

"You don't get Real by playing it safe."
— Jane Fonda

I believe that the greatest gift aging presents is the wisdom allowing us to become our most authentic selves. Over the span of my 30-year career, I've met many people—myself included—who have hidden under layers of personas. These "imposters" are there to mask the fears and the lack of nurturing we might have endured as children. We're not all victims of abusive parenting, but the vast majority of us have altered our personalities because someone, somewhere, made us feel ashamed to be who we really are.

Were you accused of being too sensitive or too outgoing? Perhaps you laughed a great deal, moved around too much, or were a social butterfly? Maybe you read or talked too much. Or maybe you had a fantastic imagination and were incredibly creative.

Sadly, it often takes just one negative comment and you decide to put away that piece of yourself that gave you joy; for some reason, it seems very important to please the critic . . . instead of staying true to yourself.

When we internalize these critical voices, we often forget about our glorious origins, and then the voices become our own. But if we choose to ignore the negative statements, if we realize that they're not relevant to us and don't define who we are, we can finally become the wise and wonderful sages we're meant to be.

The following stanza from the poem "Little Gidding" (one of the *Four Quartets*), by T. S. Eliot best expresses my belief:

> We shall not cease from exploration
> And the end of all our exploring
> Will be to arrive where we started
> And know the place for the first time.

Once our comfort levels increase, we have more energy to enter a phase of aging that psychoanalyst Erik Erikson called *generativity,* which refers to the point in our lives when we have the opportunity to become consultants, guides, mentors, or coaches to young adults in the larger society. It also means a time for community building. I've found this to be one of my greatest blessings, but it wasn't something I was capable of bringing into my life to the degree I have until I understood my own history and how it influenced my behavior. Only then was I truly able to give of myself to family, friends, and others in the way I do now.

At this moment, I'm fortunate to have the energy I need in order to live the life I've always wanted. However, I also have moments when I question the reasons for my very existence. Does it matter if I share my wisdom with audiences throughout the world? Should I have just stayed home and been the good wife and mother? Have I really done anything meaningful in my life? Will I be riddled with guilt when my mom passes? Was I a decent, caring mother? Do I have enough money to support myself through my last days, or will I have to tap dance between doorways with a tin cup in hand? Will I eventually be so short that I'll qualify as one of the munchkins in a revival of *The Wizard of Oz?* And will I ultimately forget—or care about—things ten minutes after I think about them?

As you can see, one of my saving graces is that I'm still capable of acknowledging my own absurdity. I no longer have the time to visit the islands of regret. I've ultimately realized that as long as I'm here and able, I'll continue to try to make a difference in other people's lives because that's who I am—and I'm also a survivor, just like the Italian divas of my gene pool. I'll mentor all the individuals I can, not only to encourage their talents, but also to create a legacy for mine. I'll continue to deepen my relationships with my children so they'll be left with loving memories. My grandchildren are already benefiting because our family has moved away from our dysfunctional history. They're well on their way to being succulent, savvy, and sensational.

I know that I'll do my best to look and feel as good as possible, keep my passions alive, and make sure the juices are flowing. I'll continue to work, seek love, and foster a spiritual life.

Here is a list of some of my future hopes and dreams that I'd like to share with you:

- Host a fabulous talk show for women over 50
- Write more books on juicy living
- Meet a great guy to hang out with
- Travel to exotic places with family and/or friends
- Create an institute for health, happiness, and healing
- Mentor other public speakers
- Support those who are less privileged through volunteering and fund-raising
- Continually nurture the growth of my mind, body, and spirit

What about you? What are your aspirations for the future? Have you thought about what you intend to do with the rest of your life? Below are some ideas to move into *generativity.*

Juicy Tidbits

- Become a role model, and know that your actions—or your apathy—impact the world around you. In a recent *O Magazine* article, Joan Duncan Oliver writes about the ripple effect of kind, selfless acts:

> Jonathan Haidt, Ph.D., an associate professor of psychology at the University of Virginia, . . . coined the term elevation to describe the emotion we feel when we encounter evidence of what he calls moral beauty. Seeing—or even reading about—other's courage, compassion, or generosity can not only make us better people but increase the likelihood we'll do good works of our own.

- Mentor the young people in your life, and encourage them to continue the cycle of giving. Check out what others do to inspire our youth. For example, Music legend Quincy Jones has traveled more than 400,000 miles to help young people in the

Middle East, Asia, and Africa. "We could educate all the kids on the planet for what American teens spend on cosmetics in just four months," he says. Becoming a mentor can make significant changes in helping the world become a more peaceful, loving place. For more information on mentoring, visit **www.WhoMentoredYou.org**.

- Start a giving circle. Giving circles are made up of like-minded volunteers who combine their resources, time, and energy into grant-making collectives. To check the track record of an existing group or learn more about giving circles, visit The Giving Forum at **www.givingforum.org/givingcircles**.

There are so many exciting directions to choose from and roads to follow. You merely have to look inside to discover where your heart leads you. Making a genuine difference in this world can be as simple as trying to live each day with love, kindness, and joy. I find that being playful with people not only helps to lighten their load, but my own as well.

Whatever you decide to do, make sure you use whatever time you have left in this life with as much gusto as you can possibly muster. Look within and find courage, dignity, integrity, and compassion for yourself and others. And please, kick up your heels, boots, or slippers . . . before you're too short to wear them!

ᘓᘐ ᘓᘐ ᘓᘐ ᘓᘐ ᘓᘐ ᘓᘐ

Kickin' Resources

Places to Look for More Guidance and Fun

One-Stop Shops for Body and Mind

Books

Aging Well: Surprising Guideposts to a Happier Life from the Landmark Harvard Study of Adult Development, by George E. Vaillant. Little, Brown and Company, 2002.

Aging with Attitude: Growing Older with Dignity and Vitality, by Robert Levine. Praeger Publishers, 2004.

Aging with Grace: What the Nun Study Teaches Us about Leading Longer, Healthier, and More Meaningful Lives, by David Snowdon. Bantam, 2001.

Anti-Aging Manual: The Encyclopedia of Natural Health, by Joseph B. Marion. Information Pioneers, 2003.

Baby Boomers: Can My Eighties Be Like My Fifties? (Springer Series on Lifestyles and Issues in Aging), edited by M. Joanna Mellor and Helen Rehr. Springer Publishing Company, 2005.

The Big Five-Oh! Fearing, Facing, and Fighting Fifty, by Bill Geist. William Morrow, 1997.

Chasing Life, by Sanjay Gupta, M.D. Warner Wellness, 2007.

Healthy Aging: A Lifelong Guide to Your Physical and Spiritual Well-Being, by Andrew Weil. Knopf, 2005.

Naomi's Guide to Aging Gratefully: Facts, Myths, and Good News for Boomers, by Naomi Judd. Simon & Schuster, 2007.

The New Anti-Aging Revolution: Stopping the Clock for a Younger, Sexier, Happier You!, by Ronald Klatz and Robert Goldman. Basic Health Publications, 2003.

The Power Years: A User's Guide to the Rest of Your Life, by Ken Dychtwald and Daniel J. Kadlec. John Wiley & Sons, 2005.

Websites

Anti-Aging Guide 2006 – Contains a huge amount of information on all aspects of aging, with a particular focus on anti-aging research. There's also a nutrition section with simple recipe ideas.
www.anti-aging-guide.com

Eons – Launched in 2006, Eons is a comprehensive site that inspires people to celebrate life "on the flip side of 50." It's a great community for boomers, and besides, I'm their Happiness Coach!
www.eons.com

Go60.com – An online forum for adults over 60, which tries to reimagine the possibilities of aging.
www.go60.com

Health over 50 – A comprehensive Website from the BBC, offering information and resources on all aspects of aging. Some sections, primarily those concerning social welfare benefits, will not be as interesting to American seniors, but most sections are relevant, helpful, and thoughtful.
www.bbc.co.uk/health/health_over_50

Helpguide – According to Helpguide, it's "a trusted source for non-commercial information: mental health, healthy lifestyles & aging issues." This site has—among other

things—a good, straightforward guide to nutrition.
www.helpguide.org

Holistic Health Tools: The 50+ Holistic Health Portal – Contains information, articles, tips, and discussions about a wide range of aging-related concerns, with a focus on holistic approaches to wellness.
www.holistichealthtools.com/senior.html

ThirdAge – This Website offers information on midlife health, relationships, career advice, and more.
www.thirdage.com

Adventure and Education

Books

Active Retirement for Affluent Workaholics: Planning for the Life You've Always Wanted, by Peter Silton. NP Financial Systems, 2001.

The Creaky Traveler in Ireland: Clare, Kerry, and West Cork: A Journey for the Mobile but Not Agile, by Warren Rovetch. Sentient Publications, 2006.

Cruise Vacations for Mature Travelers, by Kerry Smith. St. Martin's Griffin, 2001.

The Fit Traveler: Senior Edition, by Kari Eide and Lissa Mueller. Publishers Design Group, 2006.

Live Your Road Trip Dream: Travel for a Year for the Cost of Staying Home, by Phil and Carol White. RLI Press, 2004.

Season of Adventure: Traveling Tales and Outdoor Journeys of Women over 50, edited by Jean Gould. Seal Press, 1996.

Unbelievably Good Deals and Great Adventures That You Absolutely Can't Get Unless You're over 50 (2005–2006 edition), by Joan Rattner Heilman. McGraw-Hill, 2005.

Websites

Elderhostel – Organizes adventure holidays, focusing on offering opportunities for grandparents and their grandchildren. Provides in-depth learning experiences for people of a range of abilities.
www.elderhostel.com

ElderTreks – Organizes small group holidays to several destinations, including African safaris, traveling the Silk Road, and "exploring Mongolia by camel."
www.eldertreks.com

50plus Expeditions – This company organizes adventure trips for small groups of people who are 50+. These trips cover many destinations on all continents, including the Arctic and Antarctica.
www.50plusexpeditions.com

Senior Summer School – This company offers travel and education programs in several cities around the United States. Locations include San Diego State University, the University of Vermont, Northern Arizona University, and other universities in places such as the Appalachian Mountains, Washington State, and Wisconsin.
www.seniorsummerschool.com

Torre di Babele, The Italian Language School – Torre di Babele offers Italian language courses in Rome, Italy. The classes are international, providing participants with an opportunity to socialize with adults from around the world as they explore Rome and the Italian language and culture.
www.torredibabele.com/senior.htm

TransitionsAbroad.com, Best Senior Travel Web Sites
This Website has a lot of information on international travel and relocation. It also has a very good guide to other travel Websites of interest to people over 50.
www.transitionsabroad.com/listings/travel/senior/KeyWebSites.shtml

Arts and Culture

Books

Aging Artfully: 12 Profiles: Visual & Performing Women Artists Aged 85–105, by Amy Gorman. PAL Publishing, 2006.

Exploring Our Lives: A Writing Handbook for Senior Adults, by Francis E. Kazemek. Santa Monica Press, 2002.

Keeping the Beat: Healthy Aging Through Amateur Chamber Music Playing, by Ada P. Kahn. Wordscope Associates, 1999.

Making Your Own Mark: A Drawing and Writing Guide for Senior Citizens, by Francine Ringold and Madeline Rugh. Out on a Limb Publishing, 1990.

Seniors Acting Up: Humorous New One-Act Plays and Skits for Older Adults: An Anthology, edited by Ted W. Fuller. Pleasant Hill Press, 1996.

Writing Your Life: An Easy-to-Follow Guide to Writing an Autobiography, by Mary Borg. Cottonwood Press, 1998.

Yoga for the Brain: Daily Writing Stretches That Keep Minds Flexible and Strong, by Dawn DiPrince and Cheryl Miller Thurston. Cottonwood Press, 2006.

Websites

ArtAge Publications, The Senior Theatre Resource Center – This organization promotes seniors in theater. They run workshops; publish and distribute plays, books, and other materials; and give marketing assistance to encourage attendance and growth. They have a free newsletter. **www.seniortheatre.com**

National Center for Creative Aging (NCCA) – An organization that's dedicated to furthering an understanding of the importance of creativity to quality of life. Produces

research, lobbies for policy change, provides training and education, and disseminates information.
www.creativeaging.org

Computers and Online Communities

Books

It's Never Too Late to Love a Computer (revised edition), by Abby Stokes. Workman Publishing Company, 2005.

Windows XP for Seniors: For Senior Citizens Who Want to Start Using Computers, by Addo Stuur. Visual Steps Publishing, 2005.

Video

Computers for Seniors (and Kids of All Ages), Labrador Films, 2000.

Websites

Computers Made Easy (for senior citizens) – A Website that offers free computer training, as well as links to other sites that help educate seniors about new technologies.
http://www.csuchico.edu/~csu/seniors/computing2.html

cRANKy (The first age-relevant search engine) – A Web search engine specifically for us! It includes forums for exchanging tips and viewpoints, and making friends.
http://cranky.com

Double Nickels – An online magazine for folks over 50. Sections include Travel, Entertainment, Cooking & Recipes, Medical & Health, and many more.
www.doublenickels.com

Senior.com – An online community that enables users to communicate with friends and loved ones, shop online in a secure environment, and research a wide range of topics. **www.senior.com**

Wired Seniors – An online community with a discussion board and a radio program—a place to make friends, meet travel partners, set up home exchanges, and much more. It also features SeniorsSearch, a directory linking more than 5,000 relevant sites for the over-50 age group. **www.wiredseniors.com**

Emotional Well-Being

Books

Chicken Soup for the Grandparent's Soul: Stories to Open the Hearts and Rekindle the Spirits of Grandparents, by Jack Canfield, Mark Victor Hansen, Meladee McCarty, and Hanoch McCarty. HCI, 2002.

The Creative Age: Awakening Human Potential in the Second Half of Life, by Gene D. Cohen. HarperPaperbacks, 2001.

Living Alone & Loving It: A Guide to Relishing the Solo Life, by Barbara Feldon. Fireside, 2002.

Moving Beyond Depression: A Whole-Person Approach to Healing, by Gregory L. Jantz, with Ann McMurray. Shaw, 2003.

Saying Yes to Change: Essential Wisdom for Your Journey, by Joan Z. Borysenko, Ph.D., and Gordon F. Dveirin. Ed.D. Hay House, 2006.

Websites

Crisis, Grief & Healing – A Website with discussion boards where men and women can discuss their experience of the

grieving process. The site also has columns and articles by Tom Golden, LCSW, an expert on healing from loss.
www.webhealing.com/1grief.html

Facts About Depression in Older Adults – A fact sheet from the Public Policy Office of the American Psychological Association, including statistics and treatment options.
www.apa.org/ppo/issues/olderdepressfact.html

WidowNet – An information and self-help resource for widows and widowers of all sexual orientations. Includes a discussion forum, a place to post creative writing, and specific advice on finance and other topics of concern to seniors.
www.widownet.org

Finance, Legal Issues, and Employment

Books

The Best Home Businesses for People 50+, by Paul & Sarah Edwards. Tarcher, 2004.

Everything a Baby Boomer Should Know Before Talking to an Attorney: An Insider's Guide to Estate Planning, by Mark S. Cornwall. Baby Boomer Publishing, 2006.

The Senior Organizer: Personal, Medical, Legal, Financial, by Debby S. Bitticks, Lynn Benson, and Dorothy K. Breininger. HCI, 2006.

Websites

Senior Job Bank – A Website for job seekers over 50. There's a searchable database of available positions, and users can post résumés and create online profiles for themselves.
www.seniorjobbank.org

senior*resource*.com – An online encyclopedia for seniors with information about finance, insurance, legal issues, and other concerns.
www.seniorresource.com

Senior Service America – A nonprofit organization that provides volunteer and employment opportunities for adults over 55 who want to reenter the workforce.
www.seniorserviceamerica.org

Fitness

Books

Age Is Not a Handicap: A Complete Guide to Playing Great Golf for Seniors, by Jay Morelli. McGraw-Hill, 2005.

Fitness over Fifty: An Exercise Guide from the National Institute on Aging, by the National Institute on Aging. Hatherleigh Press, 2003.

Martial Arts after 40, by Sang H. Kim. Turtle Press, 2000.

The New Yoga for People over 50: A Comprehensive Guide for Midlife and Older Beginners, by Suza Francina. HCI, 1997.

Pilates over 50: Longer, Leaner, Stronger, Younger, by Lesley Ackland. Thorsons, 2003.

Strength Training for Seniors: How to Rewind Your Biological Clock, by Michael Fekete. Hunter House, 2006.

Strength Training over 50: Stay Fit and Fabulous, by D. Cristine Caivano. Barrons, 2005.

T'ai Chi for Seniors: How to Gain Flexibility, Strength, and Inner Peace, by Sifu Philip Bonifonte. New Page Book, 2004.

Yoga over 50: The Way to Vitality, Health, and Energy in the Prime of Life, by Mary Stewart. Fireside, 1994.

Videos

Doctor Lynn's Anti-Aging Workout for Every Body: Flex & Tone, with Lynn Anderson, 2006.

Fabulous Forever: Easy Aerobics—Slow Down Your Aging Clock, by Mirabai Holland, MFA, 2004.

Keeping Fit in Your 50s, 3-Pack (Aerobics/Strength/Flexibility), with Cindy Joseph and Robin Stuhr, 2004.

Pilates for Life: Pilates for 50+, with Amy Brown, 2005.

Website

Fifty Plus Lifelong Fitness – Spreads awareness about the importance of fitness, and sponsors events such as the Annual Fitness Weekend.
www.50plus.org

Gay, Lesbian, Bisexual, Transgender, and Transsexual Resources

Books

Golden Men: The Power of Gay Midlife, by Harold Kooden, with Charles Flowers. HarperPaperbacks, 2001.

The Intimacy Dance: A Guide to Long-Term Success in Gay and Lesbian Relationships, by Betty Berzon. Plume, 1997.

Lesbians over 60 Speak for Themselves, compiled by Monika Kehoe. Haworth Press, 1989.

Lesbian Widows: Invisible Grief, by Vicky Whipple. Harrington Park Press, 2006.

Reeling in the Years: Gay Men's Perspectives on Age and Ageism, by Tim Bergling. Southern Tier Editions, Harrington Park Press, 2004.

Whistling Women: A Study of the Lives of Older Lesbians, by Cheryl Claassen. Haworth Press, 2005.

Websites

Classic Dykes Online – This is a resource for lesbians in midlife and beyond. There are discussion boards, articles on relevant topics, peer-support lists, and an "ask an expert" section.
www.classicdykes.com

Fellowship of Older Gays (FOG) – This is a social-activities group based in San Diego, California. Their Website has many interesting links for senior gay men and lesbians.
www.geocities.com/WestHollywood/Park/9411

Gay & Lesbian Association of Retiring Persons (GLARP)
This nonprofit organization provides information and educational resources on aging for the lesbian, gay, bisexual, and transgender (LGBT) community. It's also involved in promoting the development of LGBT-friendly retirement communities.
www.gaylesbianretiring.org

Lesbian and Gay Aging Issues Network (LGAIN) – A constituent of the American Society on Aging, this organization works to raise awareness of the particular concerns of gay, lesbian, bisexual, and transgender seniors.
www.asaging.org/networks/index.cfm?cg=LGAIN

Prime Timers Worldwide – A social organization for mature gay and bisexual men, and any younger men who may be interested in meeting mature men, who come together for social, educational, and cultural activities.
www.primetimersww.org

Trans-Health.com – An online magazine that covers health and fitness from a transsexual and transgendered perspective. There's a section on aging, as well as sections

on other relevant topics such as nutrition, sexuality, disability, and emotional health.
www.trans-health.com

Retirement Communities for Gay Men and Lesbians

Carefree Communities – The Resort on Carefree Boulevard is a Florida-based housing, RV, and rental community for women. The Carefree Cove is a residential development for gays and lesbians in the Blue Ridge Mountains of North Carolina.
www.carefreecove.com and **www.resortoncb.com**

Our Town – A company that's currently developing gay and lesbian communities in various locations.
www.ourtownvillages.com

The Palms of Manasota – The first gay and lesbian retirement community located in Palmetto, Florida.
www.palmsofmanasota.com

RainbowVision Properties – RainbowVision communities are located in Santa Fe, New Mexico, and Palm Springs, California.
www.rainbowvisionprop.com

Health and Disability

Books

Complementary and Alternative Medicine for Older Adults: A Guide to Holistic Approaches to Healthy Aging, edited by Elizabeth R. Mackenzie and Birgit Rakel. Springer Publishing Company, 2006.

The Green Pharmacy Anti-Aging Prescriptions: Herbs, Foods, and Natural Formulas to Keep You Young, by James A. Duke, with Michael Castleman. Rodale Books, 2001.

The Mature Mind: The Positive Power of the Aging Brain, by Gene D. Cohen. Basic Books, 2007.

The Merck Manual of Health & Aging: The Comprehensive Guide to the Changes and Challenges of Aging—for Older Adults and Those Who Care for and about Them. Ballantine Books, 2005.

A Senior's Health Journal: A Personal Record of Vital Health and Medical Information, by Joann Lamb and Ina Yalof. St. Martin's, 2002.

Websites

MayoClinic.com, Senior Health Center – Information on healthy aging, and on diseases and conditions affecting older adults.
www.mayoclinic.com/health/senior-health/HA99999

NeuroTone – Considered physical therapy for the ears, NeuroTone is software to train the brain to counter the effects of hearing loss due to aging, long-term exposure to loud noise, and so on. Training was developed by Robert Sweetow, director of audiology at the University of California, San Francisco, Medical Center, and his colleagues. A free demonstration is available for download at **www.neurotone.com**.

NIH Senior Health – This site provides authoritative and up-to-date information on age-related health issues from the National Institutes of Health (NIH).
http://nihseniorhealth.gov

Senior Health Care – Information for older adults about health care, lifestyles, and wellness. Also includes news about geriatric research and federal and state health-care policy.
www.seniorhealthcare.org

SeniorHealthInsuranceCounseling – A Website that provides information about Medicare, Medigap, HMO, Medicaid, and Long-Term Care. This is specifically for New Yorkers, but residents of other states may find the information useful. There's also a good resources section.
www.seniorhealthinscounsel.com

Senior Health Report – News and information about health for seniors.
www.seniorhealthweek.org

WebMD, Healthy Aging Guide – Information about senior health concerns. The WebMD site also has sections on women's and men's health.
www.webmd.com/healthy-aging/guide

Home and Community

Books

Design Details for Health: Making the Most of Interior Design's Healing Potential (Wiley Series in Healthcare and Senior Living Design), by Cynthia A. Leibrock. Wiley, 2000.

The Other Way Home: A Guide for Seniors Who Live with Their Children, by Margaret Rodgers. SymPoint Communications, 2005.

Senior Cohousing: A Community Approach to Independent Living, by Charles Durrett. Ten Speed Press, 2005.

Websites

RetirementHomes.com – An online directory of retirement homes and communities, senior housing, long-term care, and elder-care facilities.
www.retirementhomes.com

Senior Home Sharing – An Illinois-based nonprofit organization that creates group homes where seniors can live together as a family.
www.seniorhomesharing.org

SeniorOutlook.com – An Internet database and information resource on senior housing that's updated daily.
www.senioroutlook.com

Just for Men

Books

The Complete Book of Men's Health: The Definitive, Illustrated Guide to Healthy Living, Exercise, and Sex, by the editors of Men's Health Books. Rodale Books, 2000.

Dr. D's Handbook for Men over 40: A Guide to Health, Fitness, Living, and Loving in the Prime of Life, by Peter Dorsen. Wiley, 1999.

The Men's Health Longevity Program: A 12-Week Plan for Bolstering Your Health, Boosting Your Brainpower, Getting Lean, Powering Up, and Adding Years to Your life, from the editors of Men's Health Books, with Kenneth A. Goldberg. Rodale Books, 2001.

Sexual Health for Men: The Complete Guide, by Richard F. Spark. Perseus Books Group, 2000.

Websites

Grumpier Old Men (GOM) – A British-based site where grumpy old men can complain about whatever aspects of the modern world are currently bothering them.
www.grumpieroldmen.co.uk

The Men's Bibliography – A free and comprehensive bibliography of writing on men, masculinities, gender, and sexualities. It includes a variety of sources, but there's a strong academic bias.
http://mensbiblio.xyonline.net

Just for Women

Books

The Art of Midlife: Courage and Creative Living for Women, by Linda N. Edelstein. Bergin & Garvey Trade, 1999.

The Five Principles of Ageless Living: A Woman's Guide to Lifelong Health, Beauty, and Well-Being, by Dayle Haddon. Atria Books, 2003.

For My Next Act . . . Women Scripting Life after Fifty, by Karen Baar. Rodale Books, 2004.

Freedoms after 50, by Sue Patton Thoele. Conari Press, 1998.

Fullness of Time: Short Stories of Women and Aging, by Martha Whitmore Hickman. Abingdon Press, 1997.

Goddesses in Older Women: Archetypes in Women over Fifty, by Jean Shinoda Bolen. HarperPaperbacks, 2002.

Going Gray, Looking Great!: The Modern Woman's Guide to Unfading Glory, by Diana Lewis Jewell. Fireside, 2004.

I'm Too Young to be Seventy: And Other Delusions, by Judith Viorst. Free Press, 2005.

Midlife Mamas on the Moon: Celebrate Great Health, Friendships, Sex, and Money and Launch Your Second Life!, by Sunny Hersh. Fast Forward Publications, 2004.

Painting the Walls Red: The Uninhibited Woman's Guide to a Fabulous Life After 40, by Judy Ford. Adams Media, 2005.

Sex and the Seasoned Woman: Pursuing the Passionate Life, by Gail Sheehy. Ballantine Books, 2007.

Women and Aging: Celebrating Ourselves, by Ruth Raymond Thone. Haworth Press, 1992.

Websites

National Association of Baby Boomer Women (NABBW) – Dotsie Bregel, founder of the popular Website **www.BoomerWomenSpeak.com**, has cooked up a new venture, designed to empower women to "find their passions and live them now."
www.nabbw.com

National Organization for Women (NOW) – Founded in 1966, NOW is the largest organization of feminist activists in the U.S. NOW campaigns for equality between the sexes and fights against discrimination and violence, among other causes.
www.now.org

Red Hat Society – A social club for women over 50.
www.redhatsociety.com

The Richard and Linda Rosenthal Center for Complementary and Alternative Medicine, Women's Health Information Resources – A list of online resources from Columbia University. The focus is academic, governmental, and clinical research oriented.
www.rosenthal.hs.columbia.edu/Women.html

Senior Women Web – A Website for women over 50, with columns and articles on a range of topics, from arts and culture, to health, money, travel, and beyond.
www.seniorwomen.com

Women over 50 – Information, insight, and meditations on aging for women over 50. This site offers book and

music recommendations and offers spiritual (but not religious) inspiration.
www.wo50.com

Women's-Wellness.com – This site is for women who are at any stage of coping with breast cancer. There's information and advice about all aspects of the experience, as well as a discussion forum.
http://womens-wellness.com/index.shtml

Nutrition

Books

The Anti-Aging Plan: Strategies and Recipes for Extending Your Healthy Years, by Roy L. Walford and Lisa Walford. Four Walls Eight Windows, 1995.

Food as Medicine: How to Use Diet, Vitamins, Juices, and Herbs for a Healthier, Happier, and Longer Life, by Dharma Singh Khalsa. Artia Books, 2003.

The Food Revolution: How Your Diet Can Help Save Your Life and Our World, by John Robbins. Conari Press, 2001.

Food: Your Miracle Medicine, by Jean Carper. HarperPaperbacks, 1998.

Stop the Clock! Cooking: Defy Aging—Eat the Foods You Love, by Cheryl Forberg. Avery, 2003.

Superfoods for Life: 250 Anti-Aging Recipes for Foods That Keep You Feeling Fit and Fabulous, by Dolores Riccio. HP Trade, 1998.

Websites

Anti Aging Nutrition News – An online newsletter with

articles about anti-aging nutrition and healthy living strategies.
www.antiagingnutritionnews.com

FoodandLife.com – Research, advice, and recipes focusing on foods that will help you age well, including targeted discussions on the positive effects of nutrition on a variety of aging-related conditions.
www.foodandlife.com

Joyful Aging – Articles and resources on nutrition, physical activity, sleep, cancer, and spiritual well-being.
www.joyfulaging.com

National Resource Center on Nutrition, Physical Activity & Aging – The center promotes active, healthy aging by working to reduce nutrition deficiencies in older adults. The site includes links to articles on nutrition and dietary guidelines and recommendations.
http://nutritionandaging.fiu.edu

The Natural Food Hub – Contains directories of edible plants and seeds, food suppliers, and discussions of whole foods.
www.naturalhub.com

Pampering Yourself

Books

Age-Defying Beauty Secrets: Look and Feel Younger Each and Every Day, by Diane Irons. Sourcebooks, 2003.

Ageless Beauty: The Secrets of Aging Beautifully, by Liz Wilde. Ryland Peters & Small, 2006.

Dr. Denese's Secrets for Ageless Skin: Younger Skin in 8 Weeks, by Adrienne Denese. Berkley Books, 2005.

Feel Fabulous Forever: The Anti-Aging Health & Beauty Bible, by Josephine Fairley and Sarah Stacey. Overlook Press, 1999.

The Handbook of Style: Expert Fashion and Beauty Advice, as told to Francine Maroukian and Sarah Woodruff. Quirk Books, 2006.

Healing Home Spa: Soothe Your Symptoms, Ease Your Pain, and Age-Proof Your Body with Pleasure Remedies, by Valerie Gennari Cooksley. Prentice Hall Press, 2003.

Lit from Within, by Victoria Moran. HarperSanFrancisco, 2004.

The RealAge Makeover: Take Years off Your Looks and Add Them to Your Life, by Michael F. Roizen. HarperCollins, 2004.

Secrets of Great Skin: The Definitive Guide to Anti-Aging Skin Care, by David J. Goldberg and Eva M. Herriott. Innova, 2005.

Wrinkle-Free Forever: The 5-Minute 5-Week Dermatologist's Program, by Howard Murad, with Dianne Partie Lange. St. Martin's Griffin, 2004.

Younger by the Day: 365 Ways to Rejuvenate Your Body and Revitalize Your Spirit, by Victoria Moran. HarperSanFransisco, 2004.

Websites

ElderStore – An family-owned online store that provides products for seniors with special needs.
www.elderstore.com

Senior Cosmetics: Anti-Aging Skin Care – Cosmetics and skin care products created especially for seniors.
www.seniorcosmetics.com

Spa Finder, Senior-Friendly Spa Vacations – A list of spas that are of particular interest to people 50 plus.
www.spafinder.com/search/results?category=194

Relationships and Sex

Books

Baby Boomer Bachelorette, or How to Have Sex at Least Once More Before You Die, by Patsy Stagner. JPS Publishing Company, 2004.

Better than Ever: Love and Sex at Midlife, by Bernie Zilbergeld, with George Zilbergeld. Crown House Publishing, 2004.

Better than I Ever Expected: Straight Talk about Sex after Sixty, by Joan Price. Seal Press, 2006.

Dr. Ruth's Sex after 50: Revving Up the Romance, Passion & Excitement!, by Dr. Ruth K. Westheimer, with Pierre A. Lehu. Quill Driver Books, 2005.

Rescue Me, He's Wearing a Moose Hat: And 40 Other Dates after 50, by Sherry Halperin. Seal Press, 2005.

Sex over 50, by Joel D. Block, with Susan Crain Bakos. Reward Books, 1999.

Still Doing It: Women and Men over Sixty Write about Their Sexuality, edited by Joani Blank. Down There Press, 2000.

Websites

ChristianSingleSeniors.com – A marriage-minded site for single Christians.
www.christiansingleseniors.com

Dating for Beginners – This site offers dating advice, and specifically addresses the issue of the suddenly single on the dating scene.
www.forbeginners.info/dating/senior-dating.htm

50YearsPlus.com – An online dating site. In addition to personal profiles, there's a chat room, an advice page, and a number of other features. Membership isn't free, but there's a free trial membership offer.
www.50yearsplus.com

Jewish Seniors Dating – A dating site for Jewish singles over 60.
www.jewishzipdating.com/seniors

Senior Datefinder – An online personals site. Membership is free.
http://seniordatefinder.com

SeniorsCircle.com – An online dating site that uses Scientific Personality Profile Analysis to match members.
http://seniorscircle.com

Government and General Advocacy Websites

Administration on Aging (AoA)
www.aoa.gov

Council for Jewish Elderly
www.cje.net

The Healthy Aging Campaign
www.healthyaging.net

National Council on Aging (NCOA)
www.ncoa.org

National Institute on Aging
www.nia.nih.gov

The Seniors Coalition
www.senior.org

SeniorsResourceGuide.com – Website of The Seniors Blue Book
www.seniorsresourceguide.com

USA.gov, Senior Citizens' Resources
www.usa.gov/Topics/Seniors.shtml

Magazines and Journals

Aging Today
Arthritis Self-Management
Arthritis Today
Focus on Healthy Aging
Journal on Active Aging
Journal of Women & Aging
Where to Retire

Gratitude to . . .

Oftentimes, books contain a page for the author to acknowledge those who have been a part of their creative journey, but the word *acknowledge* just isn't juicy enough for me. Instead, I'd like to show these individuals how grateful I am for the great joy and blessings they've brought into my life.

First and foremost, I'm grateful to my family: my sons, Jon and Erik; my daughter, Laurie; their spouses; and my grandchildren, who total 11. What a prolific group!

To my brilliant literary agent, Brian DeFiore; Louise Hay; Reid Tracy; Jill Kramer; Lisa Mitchell; and the entire amazing Hay House staff. They're fantastic, loving, and kind. How fortunate I am to be involved with these wonderful individuals!

And I'm grateful to my friends Myra, Sue and Adam, Colette, Ann, Beverly, Ken, Blair, and Will, who lovingly support and listen to me through good and bad times. And to Susan J. Cohen, LICSW, for her insight and guidance. I thank you all from the bottom of my heart.

About the Author

Loretta LaRoche, the best-selling author of *Life Is Short—Wear Your Party Pants* and *Squeeze the Day,* among other works, is an internationally renowned author and stress-management consultant who advocates humor, optimism, and resiliency as coping mechanisms. She uses her wit and wisdom to help people learn how to take stress and turn it into strength, and how to see themselves as the survivors of their own lives—that is, to find the "bless in the mess."

Loretta is a favorite with viewers of her six PBS specials, as well as on the lecture circuit, where she presents an average of 100 talks per year. She lives in Plymouth, Massachusetts.

Website: **www.LorettaLaroche.com**

Hay House Titles of Related Interest

HOW TO RUIN YOUR LIFE, by Ben Stein

THE LAST DROPOUT: Stop the Epidemic!,
by Bill Milliken

NOT SKINNY, NOT BLONDE: A Heartwrenching, Hilarious Memoir, by Monique Marvez

THE POWER OF PLEASURE: Maximizing Your Enjoyment for a Lifetime, by Douglas Weiss, Ph.D.

REPOTTING: 10 Steps for Redesigning Your Life,
by Diana Holman and Ginger Pape

SPIRALING THROUGH THE SCHOOL OF LIFE: A Mental, Physical, and Spiritual Discovery,
by Diane Ladd

THE WAY OF THE BELLY: 8 Essential Secrets of Beauty, Sensuality, Health, Happiness, and Outrageous Fun, by Neena & Veena, with Nancy Bruning

YOUR DESTINY SWITCH: Master Your Key Emotions, and Attract the Life of Your Dreams!,
by Peggy McColl

All of the above are available at your local bookstore, or may be ordered by contacting Hay House (see next page).

ও ও ও

We hope you enjoyed this Hay House book.
If you'd like to receive a free catalog featuring additional Hay House books and products, or if you'd like information about the Hay Foundation, please contact:

Hay House, Inc.
P.O. Box 5100
Carlsbad, CA 92018-5100

(760) 431-7695 or **(800) 654-5126**
(760) 431-6948 (fax) or **(800) 650-5115 (fax)**
www.hayhouse.com® • www.hayfoundation.org

ও ও ও

Published and distributed in Australia by: Hay House Australia Pty. Ltd., 18/36 Ralph St., Alexandria NSW 2015
Phone: 612-9669-4299 • *Fax:* 612-9669-4144
www.hayhouse.com.au

Published and distributed in the United Kingdom by: Hay House UK, Ltd., 292B Kensal Rd., London W10 5BE *Phone:* 44-20-8962-1230 • *Fax:* 44-20-8962-1239
www.hayhouse.co.uk

Published and distributed in the Republic of South Africa by: Hay House SA (Pty), Ltd., P.O. Box 990, Witkoppen 2068
Phone/Fax: 27-11-467-8904 • orders@psdprom.co.za
www.hayhouse.co.za

Published in India by: Hay House Publishers India, Muskaan Complex, Plot No. 3, B-2, Vasant Kunj, New Delhi 110 070
Phone: 91-11-4176-1620 • *Fax:* 91-11-4176-1630
www.hayhouse.co.in

Distributed in Canada by: Raincoast, 9050 Shaughnessy St., Vancouver, B.C. V6P 6E5 • *Phone:* (604) 323-7100
Fax: (604) 323-2600 • www.raincoast.com

ও ও ও